MATTHEW
A Devotional Commentary

BOB ROGNLIEN

FOOTSTEPS EVERY DAY, Volume One
Matthew: A Devotional Commentary

Copyright © Bob Rognlien 2023

All rights reserved. No part of this book may be reproduced without written permission, except for brief quotations in books and reviews. For information contact GX Books, bobrognlien@gmail.com or www.bobrognlien.com.

All Scripture quotations are from the Christian Standard Bible® (CSB®), Copyright © 2017 by Holman Bible Publishers. Used by permission. Christian Standard Bible® and CSB® are federally registered trademarks of Holman Bible Publishers.

Cover Design: Timothy J. Bergren
Book Design: Amit Dey
Editor: Robert Neely

ISBN: 978-0-9815247-7-1

Published by GX Books

DEDICATION

To the 135 friends who went with me
on this year-long adventure through the four Gospels.
Your insights illuminated my understanding,
your examples inspired my application,
and your companionship gave me courage to complete the journey.
May the Spirit give you grace to keep walking in Jesus' footsteps
by taking steps of faith every day.

ACKNOWLEDGEMENTS

I want to express my gratitude to all those who supported me, prayed for me, and made the writing of this book and series possible. Specifically, I want to thank Pam Rognlien, Chris Pudel, Heidi Hollings for carefully rooting out my many mistakes. Any which remain are mine alone. Thanks to Robert Neely for editing the manuscript and Amit Dey for designing the interior pages. They have both made the book eminently more readable. Special thanks to Tim Bergren for designing another great book cover. Above all I give thanks to Jesus, the Great Shepherd of the Sheep, who continues inviting us all to listen to his voice and follow him by taking steps of faith every day. To him be all the glory!

INTRODUCTION

In the first chapter of his Gospel, Mark describes Jesus' predictable pattern of spending time alone with his heavenly Father the King. *Very early in the morning, while it was still dark, he got up, went out, and made his way to a deserted place; and there he was praying.* (Mark 1:35)

Those who follow Jesus recognize this is a critical rhythm of discipleship, seeking to become more like him by hearing and responding to what he is saying every day. Paul says, *"So faith comes from what is heard, and what is heard comes through the message about Christ."* (Romans 10:17) When we listen for the voice of Jesus speaking through his written Word, the Holy Spirit plants faith in our hearts. When we exercise that faith by taking a concrete step in the footsteps of Jesus, we grow as his fruitful disciples and learn to live a more Jesus-shaped life.

Footsteps Every Day is a series of devotional commentaries on the New Testament, designed to help followers of Jesus establish a regular pattern of spending time alone with God, reading Scripture, listening in prayer, and responding with a step of faith. Volume One, *Matthew* is the first in the series and offers brief reflections on 86 passages that make up Matthew's account of Jesus' life, drawing on history, archaeology, and culture to illuminate the Way of Jesus and help you follow him with concrete steps of faith.

Each of these devotional commentaries can be read on its own at your own pace, or you can read all four Gospels in succession. If you read six passages a week, the first four volumes will take you on an incredible year-long journey through the Gospels, following the life of Jesus and reflecting on every recorded thing he said and did during his life on earth!

These books can also be used as biblical commentaries by looking up a specific passage you are studying to gain fresh insights from the historical and cultural background to inform you as you teach others and apply God's Word to daily life.

Here are my recommendations for a fruitful devotional journey in Jesus' *Footsteps Every Day*:

- Pick a time in which you have the highest likelihood of being consistent each day. Set aside at least 15 minutes, or better 30 minutes.
- Pick a place where you will be the least distracted and interrupted. Make yourself comfortable but adopt an attentive posture. Get too comfortable and you will fall asleep!
- Read the Scripture passage in your own Bible. My writing is based on the text from the Christian Standard Bible, an excellent and often overlooked translation, but you can use any version you find helpful. Read it again.
- Take some time to prayerfully listen as you scan over the passage, noting what God seems to be pointing out to you.
- Highlight important phrases and make relevant notes in the margin. (Even digital Bibles allow for this. I use the Olive Tree App.)
- Read the commentary provided in *Footsteps Every Day*.
- Prayerfully ask God what he is saying to you through all the above. Listen and write down what is coming to you in the space provided (or type it as a digital note if you are reading the eBook edition).
- Then ask God to show you the next step of faith he wants you to take.
- Write down your step of faith in the space provided (or type it as a digital note if you are reading the eBook edition).
- Take that step of faith!
- If you are having trouble taking that step, share it with someone you trust and ask them to pray for you to exercise the faith God is giving you. Take that step of faith!
- Rinse and repeat!

- "At the end of every six days, there is a section called "Footsteps Every Week." Use this space to reflect on the readings from the past week, summarize your insights from each day, identify any major themes, consider any new predictable patterns God is calling you to establish, and identify the most significant verse to memorize."

When we read God's Word and listen to what Jesus is saying to us through the Spirit, it produces faith in our hearts. Our role is to respond to what Jesus is saying by exercising that faith, taking the next step in following the footsteps of Jesus. We are not trying to change ourselves by moral willpower, but rather are putting ourselves in the place where God's Spirit can transform us from the inside out. This is what it means to live as a Jesus-shaped disciple. Please don't approach this as a religious task that you must perform but receive this opportunity as a gracious invitation to draw near to Jesus, hear his voice, and follow where he leads you on this great adventure of discipleship!

DAY 1

READ AND LISTEN: MATTHEW 1:1-17
Take a minute to listen for what the Spirit is saying in these verses…

COMMENT AND CONSIDER
The Gospel of Matthew was written by a former Jewish tax collector from Capernaum, also known by his Jewish name Levi. His life and living were completely upended when, in a shocking act of grace, Jesus called Matthew to follow him and become part of his missional family. Matthew responded to this amazing grace by giving up his lucrative but traitorous vocation of collecting exorbitant taxes from his fellow Jews on behalf of their conquering enemies the Romans. Tax collectors were despised by the local population for collaborating with their pagan occupiers, but also for lining their own pockets by extorting even higher levels of taxation than Caesar and Herod imposed. Matthew was certainly the last person anyone ever expected to be called as a disciple of a famous rabbi!

This unlikely disciple would have been trained in the secular scribal arts as well as accounting in order to manage his collection of taxes, and these skills served him well as a chronicler of Jesus' life and teaching. Right away in v. 1 we see that Matthew is writing from a Jewish perspective when he gives Jesus the title of "Christ." This means Messiah, the long-awaited King descended from David who the Prophets foretold would come to save his people and establish God's Kingdom forever. In case we missed this, Matthew adds David, the ideal Jewish king, and Abraham, the father of the Jewish people, to Jesus' heritage. He then goes on to dramatically demonstrate Jesus' historical lineage by tracing his genealogy from Abraham to Joseph, the husband of Mary.

This is not a comprehensive list of Jesus' descendants, but a selective list meant to set up Matthew's account of Jesus' life. Perhaps most striking about the list is that it contains such a variety of human beings: champions of the faith and also political villains, harlots and heroes, adulterers, Gentiles, and a pregnant virgin. It is also striking that so many women are included in this genealogy, when typical Jewish genealogies were limited to a list of male ancestors. *Tamar ... Rahab ... Ruth ... Uriah's wife ... Mary.* Matthew's inclusion of these female heroes, even prostitutes and Gentiles, prepares us for Jesus' radical inclusion of women and religious outcasts in his revolutionary movement.

Matthew begins his Gospel account by dramatically demonstrating that Jesus is the long-awaited Messiah promised by God, and that he is a King who is deeply connected to a diverse and broken humanity desperately in need of a Savior. As you begin this journey following the footsteps of Jesus through the Gospels, where do you find yourself in Jesus' genealogy? Are you an inspiring example of faithfulness to God or an unworthy sinner in need of grace? Are you someone who has always been affirmed and included in the family of God, or an outcast rejected on the basis of your gender, your upbringing, or the color of your skin? Can you see that, despite whatever lies in your own past and however others have treated you, you belong in the story of Jesus?

Reflect and Respond

What is Jesus saying to me right now?

What step of faith is Jesus calling me to take today?

DAY 2

READ AND LISTEN: MATTHEW 1:18-25

Take a minute to listen for what the Spirit is saying in these verses…

COMMENT AND CONSIDER

Matthew plunges us into the drama of Jesus' story by describing the predicament of Mary's unexpected pregnancy from Joseph's perspective. (Luke gives us Mary's perspective.) Betrothal in first century Galilee was a legally binding agreement between a couple and their families to enter marriage. About a year later this covenant was ratified by a public ceremony and a private consummation of the marriage. When Joseph learned of Mary's pregnancy, he knew he was not the father, so he naturally assumed Mary had broken their betrothal by committing adultery. The Old Testament Law was clear that a "divorce" was required in the case of adultery during betrothal, and so Joseph, being a "just" or "righteous" man planned to do just that.

Joseph had two options. He could make the reason for the divorce public, exposing Mary to the shame of social condemnation, which would ruin her future prospects for marriage and make her liable to the possibility of death by stoning. Or he could divorce her quietly, stating the reasons to as few as two or three witnesses. Joseph must have been personally hurt by this perceived unfaithfulness. Certainly, the honor/shame culture of the Middle East encouraged him to be outraged and vengeful. However, we see the strong character of this man who was willing to let Mary off easily. But Joseph was about to be stretched even further…

When he first awoke from his fitful sleep, Joseph must have chuckled at such a crazy dream: he was to complete the marriage contract because the child growing inside Mary's womb was divinely conceived and destined to save the world! And yet somehow the dream didn't fade as other dreams do. Somehow, he became increasingly convinced an angelic messenger had really been sent by the Lord to show him the way. That Joseph was willing to set aside his pride and common sense, risk ostracization by his extended family, and take the pregnant Mary as his wife speaks volumes of the faith, humility, and courage of this "righteous man."

In the 19th century, the Sisters of Nazareth bought the property on which a number of homes stood to build their new convent in the ancient center of Nazareth. Consequently, they discovered the ruins of a first-century Jewish home which archaeology and tradition indicate was most likely the house of Joseph where Jesus was raised. Surprisingly, there is a beautifully constructed tomb with a rolling stone cut into the rock beneath that home. Is this the tomb Jesus and his brothers built for their father Joseph? Perhaps it is no accident that the people who lived on that land knew of an ancient tradition that below their floors was the buried tomb of "the righteous man."

What does it mean for you to be righteous today? Are you open to the unexpected revelation of God who might be calling you to do something risky and courageous? Joseph was, and in so doing he played his part in literally saving the world!

REFLECT AND RESPOND
What is Jesus saying to me right now?

What step of faith is Jesus calling me to take today?

DAY 3

READ AND LISTEN: MATTHEW 2:1-12

Take a minute to listen for what the Spirit is saying in these verses…

COMMENT AND CONSIDER

Matthew continues to swiftly move the story of Jesus forward with a surprisingly sparse description of Jesus' birth. Unlike in Luke's account, there is no mention of the journey from Nazareth to Bethlehem, the backhanded hospitality of Joseph's extended family who refuse them the guestroom, heavenly songs of angelic hosts, or the wonder-filled adoration of smelly shepherds. All Matthew tells us is that the birth of this baby boy in Bethlehem elicits a visit from some very distant and exotic figures from the east.

The term "magi" refers to a priestly cast of Persian astrologers who searched the night skies for signs from the gods. Perhaps influenced by the messianic traditions of Jews living in the East since the Babylonian captivity, they believed a dramatic celestial phenomenon was pointing them toward the birth of a great king among the Jewish people. Even the Roman historian Suetonius was aware of the expectation of a great king who would arise from Judea to rule the world. And so, when they saw this celestial phenomenon, these learned Gentiles set off on their 900-mile journey across the inhospitable Arabian Desert bearing gifts for a Jewish king.

When the magi arrived in Jerusalem, they inquired at the massive palace of Herod, where they expected a Jewish king would be born. When they entered the palace, little did they know they were standing in the very plaza where this newborn King would one day be condemned to die. Once they heard the prophecy of Micah stating that the Messiah would be born in Bethlehem, they took the short four-mile trek south to this seemingly insignificant village, the hometown of King David. As the magi continued to study the celestial phenomenon in the sky over Bethlehem, they identified a particular house, the extended family home of Joseph's relatives where he and Mary still resided after Jesus' birth.

It is hard to overstate the turmoil caused by the arrival of the magi at the home of Joseph's relatives or the shock that their stated purpose would have evoked. Did respect for their learning and position overcome the Jewish reticence to invite these "unclean" Gentiles into their home? Did the magi's worship of the baby Jesus offend the family's biblical sensibilities about idolatry? Did the royal gifts offered to their son confirm the message Mary and Joseph had already received from angels and shepherds that Jesus was the long-awaited Jewish Messiah?

We don't have clear answers to these questions, but we do know that God used these foreign pagan astrologers to demonstrate the true meaning of Jesus' birth: the King of kings has come! What is your response to the birth of Jesus? Are you willing to follow God's leading wherever his Spirit takes you? Are you open to receiving the surprising messengers he may send to show you the way? Are you ready to worship him by offering all that you are to him? What does the visit of these mysterious magi say to you today?

REFLECT AND RESPOND

What is Jesus saying to me right now?

What step of faith is Jesus calling me to take today?

DAY 4

READ AND LISTEN: MATTHEW 2:13-23
Take a minute to listen for what the Spirit is saying in these verses…

COMMENT AND CONSIDER
Naturally the magi's intended destination was Jerusalem, home of the kings of Israel, and their inquiries touched a nerve in the aging and increasingly paranoid despot, so-called Herod "the Great." A politically savvy puppet-king beholden to the Romans, Herod thought he would manipulate the magi into identifying this newborn king for him so he could eliminate his potential rival. But the true King was unfolding a plan not even Herod could foil!

In the final years of his life, Herod's growing fear that those around him were plotting to overthrow and murder him prompted heinous acts of violence, even to the point of executing three of his own sons. And so, Matthew's account of the unthinkable slaughter of the innocent boys of Bethlehem is painfully credible, while still unimaginably evil. About ninety years later, the Apostle John received a vision that included a terrible dragon who was waiting to devour "a male child, one who is to rule all the nations with a rod of iron," but God preserved the life of the newborn King and his mother fled "into the wilderness." (See Revelation 12:4-6.)

Whatever the meaning of this vision might be, it is clear from Matthew's account that the powers of darkness were colluding with deeply corrupt human agents in a horrendous attempt to wipe out Jesus as a baby before he could even begin to fulfill his epic mission. And yet we see that nothing catches God by surprise! He is fully aware of the enemy's schemes and is faithful to guide, equip, and empower his children to face and overcome even the greatest of attacks.

Joseph had learned how to recognize and follow God's guidance, even through angelic messengers and prophetic dreams, and now it was serving him and his little family well in the midst of the battle. In the Roman period, Egypt was a well-connected part of the Empire with a sizable Jewish population, but it was outside Herod's jurisdiction. So traveling there to escape the bloodthirsty tyrant's wrath made perfect sense. Again, God's prophetic direction let them know when it was safe to return to Israel, although the even more chaotic rule of Herod's son Archelaus was a good reason to return to Mary's hometown of Nazareth in the north rather than Joseph's family in Bethlehem, just four miles south of Jerusalem.

Perhaps it was from Joseph that the boy Jesus first saw an example of someone listening and responding to God's prompting. Later Jesus would say, *"Truly I tell you, the Son is not able to do anything on his own, but only what he sees the Father doing. For whatever the Father does, the Son likewise does these things."* (John 5:19)

Are you equipped for the spiritual battle you will inevitably face as you follow Jesus? Are you learning to listen for the voice of your King, however he chooses to reveal himself? Will you trust him enough to follow his guidance wherever he leads you as Joseph and Mary did?

REFLECT AND RESPOND
What is Jesus saying to me right now?

What step of faith is Jesus calling me to take today?

DAY 5

READ AND LISTEN: MATTHEW 3:1-17

Take a minute to listen for what the Spirit is saying in these verses…

COMMENT AND CONSIDER

Matthew picks up the story of Jesus some twenty-eight years later as he was leaving his hometown of Nazareth and heading south through the Jordan Valley to the place at the Jordan River where his relative John was causing a huge stir. Just east of Jericho, John was challenging people from all walks of life to be immersed in the water as a sign of their repentance. He was crystal clear about his mission: John was preparing the way for the coming Messiah by calling people to turn their hearts back to God so they would be ready to receive their true King.

John instinctively knew Jesus did not need to repent and therefore was confused by Jesus' request for baptism. But Jesus knew he needed to set an example for others to follow, and so he stepped into the waters of the Jordan. When Jesus told John this was to *"fulfill all righteousness,"* he used covenantal language to indicate his fulfilment of God's promise through the prophet Jeremiah, *"I will make a new covenant with the house of Israel and the house of Judah …I will put my teaching within them and write it on their hearts. I will be their God, and they will be my people."* (Jeremiah 31:31-33) The events that followed demonstrated what kind of Covenant Jesus was inaugurating.

First the heavens were opened, and the Spirit was poured out on Jesus. In this New Covenant, God is present to his people in a new, intimate, and enduring way through the abiding presence of his Spirit. Second, God declared Jesus' identity as the Son who is fiercely and unconditionally loved by his Father. In this New Covenant, we are restored to our true identity as the daughters and sons of God by the power of Jesus' grace and love. In Jesus' baptism we see the truth about ourselves revealed in our baptism. We are the beloved children of our heavenly Father who have been made one with him through baptism into the New Covenant of Jesus!

When we step into the waters of baptism, God reveals the same truth about you and me that he revealed in Jesus' baptism. The question is: are we ready to receive that unconditional love through the Holy Spirit and live in that restored identity as sons and daughters of God? The place where John baptized Jesus was recently opened to visitors, so we can now step into the river in the very place where this momentous event took place. But you don't have to travel to the Jordan River to receive God's great love for you. You don't need to be immersed in the Jordan to reclaim your identity as a child of God.

Right now, wherever you are sitting reading these words, your heavenly Father is pouring his endless love into your heart through the Holy Spirit and declaring the most fundamental truth about you: "You are my beloved daughter! You are my beloved son! I am so proud of you! I am so pleased with you!" Will you turn your heart to him and receive this great love? Will you claim your true identity as a beloved child of the Heavenly Father?

Reflect and Respond

What is Jesus saying to me right now?

What step of faith is Jesus calling me to take today?

DAY 6

READ AND LISTEN: MATTHEW 4:1-11

Take a minute to listen for what the Spirit is saying in these verses...

COMMENT AND CONSIDER

Why does the Holy Spirit lead Jesus into the desert following his baptism? We know God does not tempt us—that is the devil's purview. So why did the Spirit lead Jesus into this time of isolation and fasting? The same Greek word can be translated "tempted" or "tested." The purpose of temptation is to cause someone to fail. The purpose of testing is to establish someone in what they have learned. The Father's purpose for Jesus in the desert was to prepare him for the battle that lies ahead. The devil's purpose in the desert was to try and stop Jesus before he can start. Both apply to our walk with Jesus as well.

When you visit the site of Jesus' baptism in the Jordan River and look west, you see the imposing mountains of the Judean Desert rising up toward Jerusalem, riven by countless dry valleys (wadis). The most prominent of these desert valleys is Wadi Qelt, which empties into the Jordan valley just south of the ancient city of Jericho. This wadi is unique both for its dramatic depth and because there are three springs that bring life to what is otherwise a harsh and barren desert landscape. It is easy to picture Jesus following the Spirit's leading west and passing Jericho before disappearing into the Judean Desert.

The devil typically attacks us where we are most vulnerable, so it is when Jesus is physically weakened by his fasting that the devil takes a run at Jesus. First, he goes after Jesus' natural human desire to fill the emptiness inside of him with something besides God—namely bread. Then he appeals to the human desire for approval and recognition. Finally, he tries to feed the human desire for power and control. These three temptations can be described as Appetite, Approval, and Ambition. By which of these are you most prone to be tempted? (Pick one now.)

We must not miss the devil's strategy. He repeatedly says, *"If you are the Son of God…"* If he could undermine Jesus' identity as the beloved Son of God, Satan knew he would prevent Jesus from operating in the royal authority that comes from knowing his Father is the King of the Universe. The same is true for each of us. If we are deceived about our identity, we will never be able to exercise the authority given to us by our Father the King to represent him and do his will on earth as it is done in heaven. Do you know who you really are, who God has declared you are?

Notice Jesus' strategy for overcoming the devil: he does not speak on his own authority, but he speaks the Word of God as an authorized representative of his Father the King. Jesus is showing us how we can overcome the enemy of our soul and learn to live by the power of the Spirit to do the will of God. When you face the deceiver's attack, claim your true identity as a daughter/son of your Father, King of the Universe. Speak the Word of God as an authorized representative of the King. Tell the devil to go and he will flee. Are you ready to exercise the authority you have been given?

Reflect and Respond

What is Jesus saying to me right now?

What step of faith is Jesus calling me to take today?

Footsteps Every Week: Review

Write a brief summary of what Jesus said to you each day this past week and the step of faith he called you to take:

Monday

Tuesday

Wednesday

Thursday

Friday

Saturday

Footsteps Every Week: Reflect

Big Picture

As you look over what Jesus has said to you this past week, do you see any themes? What is the most important thing you need to remember and believe?

Predictable Pattern

As you look over what Jesus called you to do this past week, is there a new predictable pattern he is inviting you to establish in your life with God and others?

Plant the Word

As you look over the readings from this past week, write out the passage that feels most important for you and memorize it over the next week:

DAY 7

Read and Listen: Matthew 4:12-25
Take a minute to listen for what the Spirit is saying in these verses...

Comment and Consider
Both Matthew and Mark tell us the arrest of his relative John the Baptist by Herod Antipas caused Jesus to depart the southern region of Israel, where he was baptized and tempted, and return to Galilee in the north. Luke tells us Jesus returned to his hometown of Nazareth, where he declared the shocking message that God's long-awaited messianic Kingdom was finally beginning. Sadly, he was profoundly rejected, not only by the people of his hometown, but by his own extended family. For this reason, Jesus left Nazareth and moved to Capernaum, a medium-sized fishing town on the north shore of the Sea of Galilee where he had met some potential friends. Matthew quotes Isaiah 9:1-2 which foretells this exact geographical context for the great messianic light that would one day begin to shine in the darkness.

In Capernaum Jesus began to proclaim a revolutionary message that Matthew liked to call *"the good news of the kingdom."* The Kingdom of God is the long-awaited promise that God will one day enter into his broken creation and reestablish his righteous rule through his anointed King (Hebrew: "Messiah," Greek: "Christ"). He was essentially saying heaven is coming to earth! When Jesus said, *"Repent, because the kingdom of heaven has come near,"* it was an invitation to begin living according to the reality of this heavenly rule rather than the rulers of this earth and the prince of darkness.

John the Baptist was the first to announce this Good News (Matthew 3:2), but now Jesus took the baton further when he said, *"follow me."* He was not only calling people to a new Kingdom mindset (*"repent"*), but he was inviting them into a whole new Kingdom way of life through a relationship with him (*"follow me"*). This relationship is of a disciple to a rabbi, in which the rabbi not only teaches his followers truths they can learn (information) but also models a way of life they can follow (imitation). It was through this kind of discipling relationship that Jesus invited them to learn how to live as part of God's coming Kingdom. He also challenged them to invite others to enter that same Kingdom by following them as they followed Jesus.

These four fishermen decided to leave their family business and follow Jesus fulltime, which could lead us to assume they were poor peasants who had nothing better to do. But, in fact, the archaeology tells a different story. Based on the remains of Simon and Andrew's extended family home in Capernaum, we know these fishing families had a very good life in a beautiful place. But the invitation Jesus offered was such Good News, and the way of life he was modeling was so much better, that these successful business owners decided to leave their lucrative business behind in order to learn this new way of life Jesus was offering them.

What about you? Have you caught Jesus' startling vision of the coming Kingdom of God? Do you recognize his way of life is better than the one you can make for yourself? Is this News good enough for you to leave behind your old way of life and enter into a discipling relationship which helps you learn to follow Jesus' Way? Are you willing to invite others to imitate you as you imitate him?

REFLECT AND RESPOND
What is Jesus saying to me right now?

What step of faith is Jesus calling me to take today?

DAY 8

READ AND LISTEN: MATTHEW 5:1-16
Take a minute to listen for what the Spirit is saying in these verses…

COMMENT AND CONSIDER
The four Gospel accounts of Jesus' life are not written in a strictly chronological order. Each one has its own emphasis and outline based on the message God inspired for a particular community. In his Gospel, Matthew emphasizes the ways Jesus fulfilled the prophecies of the Hebrew Scriptures. He organized Jesus' teaching into five blocks, like Moses' writing of the law was divided into the five books of the Torah. It is almost as though Matthew is presenting Jesus as a new Moses who came to lead God's people into the ultimate promised land. The extraordinary passage we are reading today is the introduction to the first of these five blocks of teaching, often called the Sermon on the Mount. The hill which rises above Capernaum with sweeping views of the Sea of Galilee historically has been identified as the place where Jesus delivered this teaching. His references to birds and lilies seem to fit that setting perfectly.

Jesus began with eight declarations of blessedness. The first (v. 3) and the last (v. 10) promise that *"the kingdom of heaven is theirs."* In Hebrew poetry, the opening and closing line define the context for what comes between. These eight statements of blessing are Jesus' way of describing how things work in the Kingdom of heaven, and they are quite surprising. In the kingdoms of this world, the poor are despised, those who mourn are pitied, and the hungry are left wanting. Jesus said in God's Kingdom they are blessed. In the kingdoms of this world, the humble are stepped on, the merciful are taken for fools, and the pure in heart are taken advantage of by the impure. Jesus said in God's Kingdom they are blessed. Peacemakers and the persecuted are dismissed as idealists, but in God's Kingdom they are blessed.

Jesus' point is that things work differently in the Kingdom of heaven than they do in the kingdoms of this world. The difference is the citizens of God's

Kingdom have a source of blessing that is not based on circumstance. The Greek word translated "blessed" in these verses is *makaroi,* which describes a transcendent joy which does not come from our circumstances, but from our connection to the God who loves us unconditionally and is in the process of working all things together for our good. (See Romans 8:28.)

This kind of indestructible joy is the blessing Paul and Silas felt when they sang hymns of praise to God after being beaten and thrown into the stocks in Philippi. (See Acts 16:25.) Paul described this non-circumstantial blessing when he wrote to the Philippians from another prison, *"In any and all circumstances I have learned the secret of being content—whether well fed or hungry, whether in abundance or in need. I am able to do all things through him who strengthens me."* (Philippians 4:12-13)

Jesus went on to say that this kind of indestructible joy is like the salt that preserves our food and makes it taste better; it shines like the light of a city on a hill that cannot be hid, like a lamp set up on a stand. What would it look like for you to follow Jesus deeper into this Kingdom of Heaven? What would it look like to live a life where your blessedness is not based on circumstances, but on your connection to the Father? How is God calling you to shine the light of this Kingdom blessing on those who are in darkness?

Reflect and Respond

What is Jesus saying to me right now?

What step of faith is Jesus calling me to take today?

DAY 9

READ AND LISTEN: MATTHEW 5:17-26
Take a minute to listen for what the Spirit is saying in these verses...

COMMENT AND CONSIDER
In classic rabbinical style, Jesus cited various laws from the Old Testament, but instead of quoting the interpretation of other rabbis, he radically intensified their meaning through his own new interpretation. Murder is not just taking someone's physical life, but anything we say that diminishes their identity as a beloved child of God! Adultery is not just sex outside of marriage, but even imagining it with someone besides your spouse!

It is easy to read these words and assume Jesus is setting up a stringent new legal system for his followers, and that we need to follow these rules in order to be in right relationship with God. Nothing could be further from the truth. Jesus constantly criticized the Pharisees for their legalism and hypocrisy, demonstrating instead God's gracious embrace of so-called "sinners." On the other hand, Jesus made it clear he did not come to do away with the Law or the Prophets. As he said in verse 17, *"I did not come to abolish but to fulfill."* This word *"fulfill"* is the same word he used with John when he said his baptism was *"to fulfill all righteousness."* (Matthew 3:15)

What does it mean for Jesus to "fulfill" the Law and Prophets? The Greek word literally means to fill something more completely. Jesus filled ritual bathing with greater meaning by adopting baptism as the demonstration of our identity as children of God in the New Covenant of grace. Now Jesus was filling the Law with new meaning by showing us it is a descriptor of life in the Kingdom of Heaven.

To do this, he intensified the moral demand of the Law by calling us to inwardly embody the outward principle expressed in each Law, rather than just externally obeying the letter of the Law as the Pharisees were prone to do. This is a mark of the New Covenant foretold by Jeremiah when God said, *"I will put my teaching within them and write it on their hearts."* (Jeremiah 31:33) It wasn't only Jesus' teaching that fulfilled the Law, but also the life he lived. Jesus perfectly embodied his new vision of the Law, both inwardly and outwardly, as a demonstration of the Kingdom of Heaven.

If we try to live up to this vision of the Kingdom through our own moral willpower, we will fall miserably short and will be liable to the religious legalism and two-faced hypocrisy of the Pharisees. If we embrace Jesus' vision of a Kingdom where we live in inward and outward harmony with the will of God and yet admit that we cannot live up to that vision by our own strength, we will be in a good place to receive the grace which alone can transform us from the inside out.

The key to reading the Sermon on the Mount as a Jesus-shaped disciple is refusing to compromise the vision of living according to the Kingdom in which God's perfect will is done on earth as it is in heaven, while at the same time recognizing our daily need for God's grace and the power of his Spirit to shape us one step of faith at time more into the image of Jesus. How do you see the Kingdom of Heaven demonstrated in the life of Jesus? How is your relationship with Jesus helping you to live into that vision today?

Reflect and Respond

What is Jesus saying to me right now?

What step of faith is Jesus calling me to take today?

DAY 10

READ AND LISTEN: MATTHEW 5:27-42

Take a minute to listen for what the Spirit is saying in these verses…

COMMENT AND CONSIDER

It is hard to imagine a moral challenge greater than the one we find in these verses. Who does not lapse into lust with their eyes? Who has not added an oath to their yes or no? The current divorce rate in North America is over 50 percent, even among professing Christians, most of whom go on to marry again. And how are we ever to find the courage and grace to submit to those who persecute us?

Jesus showed us by his example what it looks like to live according to the principles of heaven, even while we live in a fallen and broken world. It is challenging and costly to follow Jesus and live as a part of his Kingdom, because the Kingdom of Heaven inevitably comes into conflict with the kingdoms of this world. We will never be able to face and overcome that costly challenge by our own strength, which is why it is so important that we learn to walk by faith with Jesus and allow his Spirit to transform us day by day into his image.

In verses 29-30 Jesus gives a very vivid picture of how to deal with temptations: by amputating the offending member of our body! While this is obviously a metaphor, Jesus' point is clear. It is critical that we remove from our lives those things that lead us away from God's Kingdom and entangle us in sin. What potential traps and roadblocks can you remove from your life to keep you on track following Jesus?

In verse 37 Jesus challenges us not to try and assure people of our honesty and integrity by adding unnecessary promises, but to let the example of our lives make a simple "yes" and a simple "no" enough. What is the language you need to prune from your vocabulary in order to bear more and better fruit that lasts?

In verse 39 Jesus calls us not to resist those who are treating us unjustly by defending ourselves. In our flesh we respond that we have the right to slap those who slap us, to mount a defense against those who sue us, to refuse those who try and force us to do more than we are obligated to do, and to say no to those who want what we have. It is true we have these rights in the kingdoms of this world, but in the Kingdom of heaven we are called to give up our rights for the sake of others. What is one area of your life where Jesus is calling you to stop trying to defend your rights and to give as freely as you have received?

Remember: Don't try to respond to these challenges by summoning your own strength and willpower. Instead, draw near to Jesus, yield to his Spirit, listen to what he is saying to you, and then respond by exercising the faith he is giving you.

Reflect and Respond

What is Jesus saying to me right now?

What step of faith is Jesus calling me to take today?

DAY 11

READ AND LISTEN: MATTHEW 5:43-6:4
Take a minute to listen for what God is saying in these verses...

COMMENT AND CONSIDER
Now we have reached the pinnacle of the moral Mount Everest Jesus has called us to climb! Genuinely loving our enemies and praying for those who persecute us certainly requires divine perfection. As Jesus points out, it is easy to love those who love us. In fact, love begets love. Even *"tax collectors"* (think: the worst person you can imagine) are able to respond to love with love.

But loving those who don't love us is a different story. If we try to love them by our own strength, that well will run dry soon enough. If we ever hope to love unconditionally, we must tap into a source of love greater than ourselves. As we come to know more fully in Jesus the God who is love, and open ourselves to his Spirit, we discover we are connected to the Source of infinite, unconditional, and never-ending love! Paul said, *"God's love has been poured out in our hearts through the Holy Spirit who was given to us."* (Romans 5:5) John said it this way, *"We love because he first loved us."* (1 John 4:19)

Here the point is the same. If we try to love others by our own strength, we will fall short. If we allow the Holy Spirit to pour his endless love into our hearts, that love will transform us from the inside out. There can be no higher calling than Jesus' admonition in verse 48, *"Be perfect, therefore, as your heavenly Father is perfect."* The only way we will ever come close that towering Himalayan peak is to keep our eyes on Jesus, keep our ears tuned to his voice, and keep following where he leads us on this adventure of discipleship one step of faith at a time.

In chapter six, Jesus' Sermon on the Mount turns from his vision for the Kingdom as found in the Law to guidance on how to grow in the basic spiritual disciplines of giving, praying, and fasting. First, he addresses our motivation. If we engage in these spiritual practices in order to receive admiration and affirmation from others, we have completely missed the point.

The Pharisees loved to receive public recognition for their religious observances. There was a place at the Temple in Jerusalem where people could donate their alms for the poor by dropping them in trumpet-shaped bronze funnels that led to the underground Temple treasury. The sound of those coins rattling down into the vault were like a trumpet announcing how much was being given! Jesus warns us that such acts of charity are spiritually empty and only lead to hypocrisy, like the actors who hid behind masks in the Greek theater.

Spiritual disciplines are designed to help us intentionally draw nearer to the God who has so freely poured out his love on us. The appropriate motivation for spiritual disciplines is a desire to draw closer to this God of love so that we might know and love him more. The result of this growing intimacy is a greater capacity to love others and do God's will on earth as it is done in heaven.

Do you desire to draw closer to the Father? What secret act of generosity can you carry out this week that would help you grow in the Father's love?

Reflect and Respond
What is God saying to me right now?

What step of faith is God calling me to take today?

DAY 12

READ AND LISTEN: MATTHEW 6:5-18
Take a minute to listen for what the Spirit is saying in these verses…

COMMENT AND CONSIDER
Prayer is the primary spiritual discipline that helps us draw near to the Father's heart and learn to keep in step with his Spirit. When we use ostentatious language in our prayers, our spiritual pride grows rather than our relationship with God. When we pray to gain public recognition, we find ourselves further from the Father, not closer. The same is true with fasting and giving for public recognition. The antidote Jesus offers for this mistake is to do our spiritual exercises secretly so that no one but God knows what we are up to. This does not mean we should never pray or fast or give in public, but it is good to periodically check our heart in this way for creeping spiritual pride and hypocrisy.

In verse 9 Jesus offers a model prayer for his disciples. Luke tells us the original setting of this prayer was when the disciples saw Jesus praying and asked him to teach them how to pray. (See Luke 11:1.) This is how discipleship works. We observe the example of our rabbi, we receive training from our rabbi, then we grow by imitating our rabbi. Our Rabbi Jesus is training us to pray as he prays, not by giving us a rote prayer to repeat, but an outline of how to pray.

These are the six model petitions he gives us:

- *"Our Father in heaven, your name be honored as holy."* Jesus-shaped prayer recognizes and honors God as our loving Father.
- *"Your kingdom come. Your will be done on earth as it is in heaven."* Jesus-shaped prayer recognizes our Father as the true King of the Universe and seeks to know and do his will.

- *"Give us today our daily bread."* Jesus-shaped prayer is bold to ask our loving Father the King for provision, trusting him to provide what we truly need.
- *"And forgive us our debts, as we also have forgiven our debtors."* Jesus-shaped prayer recognizes our need for forgiveness, expresses trust in the gracious nature of our Father the King who forgives, and offers the same grace to those who have wronged us.
- *"And do not bring us into temptation."* Jesus-shaped prayer looks to our Father the King for guidance, so we do not walk into the snares of the enemy but stay on the path of righteousness.
- *"Deliver us from the evil one."* Jesus-shaped prayer actively engages in spiritual warfare knowing we carry the authority of our Father the King, and trusts in his power to overcome the enemy.

With which of these six types of prayer are you most comfortable? Which ones are the least familiar to you?

If we are going to learn to pray as our Rabbi Jesus prays, we will practice all six types of prayer that he models for us. You can try spending a few minutes praying in each of these ways. You can focus on one of these types of prayer each day of the week. You can pray each of the petitions Jesus gave us and ask the Holy Spirit to show you which type of prayer to focus on in that moment.

REFLECT AND RESPOND

What is Jesus saying to me right now?

What step of faith is Jesus calling me to take today?

Footsteps Every Week: Review

Write a brief summary of what Jesus said to you each day this past week and the step of faith he called you to take:

Monday

Tuesday

Wednesday

Thursday

Friday

Saturday

Footsteps Every Week: Reflect

Big Picture

As you look over what Jesus has said to you this past week, do you see any themes? What is the most important thing you need to remember and believe?

Predictable Pattern

As you look over what Jesus called you to do this past week, is there a new predictable pattern he is inviting you to establish in your life with God and others?

Plant the Word

As you look over the readings from this past week, write out the passage that feels most important for you and memorize it over the next week:

DAY 13

READ AND LISTEN: MATTHEW 6:19-34
Take a minute to listen for what the Spirit is saying in these verses…

COMMENT AND CONSIDER
Our modern western society is built on the pursuit of material gain. We are constantly told we need various products to be fulfilled. It is nearly impossible to escape the influence of our highly materialistic culture. Money and possessions are the most common idols in the modern world. This is not a new phenomenon. In Jesus' time the rabbis taught material wealth was a sign of God's blessing, so the pursuit of material wealth was spiritualized. The assumption was, "If I become rich, I will gain God's favor. If I am wealthy, I must be better than others." We can hear the same twisted theology from the pulpits of prosperity preachers today!

Jesus offers a radically different view of life. He tells us our value and meaning cannot be measured by our possessions. He warns us that material wealth is fleeting and fragile, subject to moths, rust, and thieves. Even more he shows us that money will compete with our allegiance to God and seek to enslave us. The bottom line is that we will have to choose which we serve, God or money. In the end whatever we decide is most valuable will ultimately define us. As Jesus says, *"For where your treasure is, there your heart will be also."*

The traditional location for this Sermon on the Mount (Matthew 5-7) is the hillside that rises above Capernaum and overlooks the north shore of the Sea of Galilee. When you stand on this hillside in the spring, it can be covered with beautiful wildflowers. Nearly any time of year, you will see countless birds flying overhead due to the abundance of the ecosystem surrounding the lake. I am pretty sure Jesus was pointing at the birds and the flowers when he used them as an illustration of God's incredible faithfulness to provide for his children!

When we put too much emphasis on material possessions, we set ourselves up for a life of anxiety. We worry about having enough. We worry about having the right things. We worry about losing what we have. Jesus shows us it is a question of where we are placing our trust. If we put our faith in our things, we will live a very precarious life. If we put our faith in God, we will find security, peace, and fruitfulness. Instead of living in fear and being driven to constantly pursue material gain, Jesus shows a better way. He left his lucrative family business and his comfortable family home to fulfill the Father's purpose, relying on God for everything he needed. This freed him to focus his life completely on seeking God's Kingdom.

This doesn't mean everyone is called to quit their jobs and sell their house. It does mean those who follow Jesus will choose to trust the Father for provision so we can focus our lives on seeking God's Kingdom first. Freedom from fear and anxiety over material possessions sets us free to center our lives around doing God's will on earth as it is in heaven. Paradoxically, this is how we receive every other thing we need or long for! In what area of your life is God calling you to trust him to provide? What does it mean for you to seek God's Kingdom first today?

Reflect and Respond

What is Jesus saying to me right now?

What step of faith is Jesus calling me to take today?

DAY 14

READ AND LISTEN: MATTHEW 7:1-12
Take a minute to listen for what the Spirit is saying in these verses…

COMMENT AND CONSIDER
The Pharisees positioned themselves as experts in the Law who interpreted and applied that Law in daily life. While they enthusiastically applied that Law to others and pronounced judgment over those who did not fit their interpretation, they often failed to apply these same principles to themselves. Jesus shows us how ridiculous this attitude is when he likens the judging of others to ignoring a plank in our own eye while trying to point out a tiny splinter in someone else's eye. Jesus uses the word "hypocrite" to describe this posture, which is the same word used to describe the actors in Greek theater who wore exaggerated masks to portray certain characters. These masks would have been used routinely in the large theater that stood in Sepphoris, the Roman-style Jewish city just a few miles from Jesus' hometown of Nazareth.

Jesus has already told us that the secret to a truly fruitful life is seeking God's Kingdom above all else. (See Matthew 6:33.) Now he is telling us how to seek that Kingdom. Asking is the initiation of that search in prayer, seeking is following the direction which comes from that request, and knocking is the determination to persevere until God opens the door. We completely miss Jesus' point if we try to turn this into a formula to get what we want. Jesus is telling us we seek first the Kingdom of God by asking for his will to be done, searching out where his will leads us, and then pressing in by faith in the particular area to which he leads us until we see heaven break into earth!

We are to enter this prayerful search for the Kingdom with confidence, knowing we have a good Father who wants good for us. When we ask for what is good (bread, fish) he won't give us what is bad (stone, snake). Likewise, if we walk according to our will rather than his and ask for something contrary to his will (stone, snake), he won't give us what we ask for. The whole point of prayer is to align our will with God's will, not to get God lined up with our will. This is why submitted prayer is critical to a life of seeking God's Kingdom. As we ask, seek, and knock for his will to be done on earth as it is in heaven, we will find ourselves more and more living as a part of his coming Kingdom.

If we follow our own will and seek our own kingdom, we will end up like the Pharisees, hypocrites who judge others while ignoring our own sin. We will end up praying for our own will to be done rather than God's which is always infinitely better. This is like giving your steak dinner to stray dogs or dumping your finest jewelry into the trough to be devoured by pigs! Instead, Jesus is teaching us to live according to the prayer he taught us to pray, *"Your kingdom come, your will be done, on earth as it is in heaven."* Are you asking, seeking, and knocking on the door of your kingdom or God's? Are you applying the principles of God's Kingdom to yourself, or are you focused on trying to fix everyone else's life?

Reflect and Respond
What is Jesus saying to me right now?

What step of faith is Jesus calling me to take today?

DAY 15

READ AND LISTEN: MATTHEW 7:13-23
Take a minute to listen for what the Spirit is saying in these verses…

COMMENT AND CONSIDER

Jesus said, *"I am the gate"* and *"I am the way…"* (John 10:9, 14:6). Entering the life Jesus offers and following that way of life are not easy or comfortable and therefore will not be popular. The wide gate and broad road are the way of this world, and so lead us into the kingdoms of this world. While it can seem good at the time, ultimately this way leads to the destruction of all that we hope for. But when we put our trust in Jesus and decide to let him guide and shape our lives, we find ourselves on a road that leads us into the fruitful and meaningful life we were meant to live. This is the Kingdom of God!

During Jesus' lifetime and the time of his first disciples, a number of charismatic figures gained popularity in Israel but ultimately led their followers into devastating destruction—people like Judas the Galilean, Theudas the rebel, the prophet from Egypt, and Jesus son of Hananiah. In these verses Jesus of Nazareth teaches us how to discern between those who will lead us into God's Kingdom on the narrow path and those who will lead us into destruction on the wide path. He tells us to be careful because these false prophets will try to adopt the outward attributes of true prophets, like wolves wearing sheep's clothing.

Jesus explains that the way to discern the character of a leader is to look at the fruit of their lives. Good fruit does not come from a diseased tree. Some will try to tie good fruit onto their branches to mimic a good tree. They may even be able to put on an impressive show by counterfeiting spiritual gifts like prophecy, deliverance, and apparent miracles. But do you see genuine love, joy, peace, patience, kindness, goodness, faithfulness, gentleness, and self-control naturally overflowing from their deep, personal walk with God? Are these godly character traits leading them to do the will of God, even when no one else is looking? If so, this is a good sign that they are a reliable guide to the narrow way of Jesus.

Jesus didn't sugarcoat the nature of God's Kingdom. He was clear that following him, doing the will of God on earth as it is done in heaven, will bring you into direct conflict with the kingdoms of this world and the kingdom of darkness which stands behind them. This is why Jesus told us that being his disciple means taking up our cross and following his way, which is narrow and difficult compared to the way of the world.

To find that way and follow that road, we will need help. We will need mentors who are ahead of us on the journey to help show us the way. They don't need to be perfect, but they need to be genuine and on the right track. This is how we in turn can help others enter through the narrow gate by putting their trust in Jesus. This is how we can become guides for others who are behind us on this narrow road. This is what it means to be a disciple who makes disciples. Have you entered through the narrow gate? Are you following the narrow road? Who is helping you follow Jesus' way? Who are you helping find that way with you?

Reflect and Respond

What is Jesus saying to me right now?

What step of faith is Jesus calling me to take today?

DAY 16

READ AND LISTEN: MATTHEW 7:24-8:4
Take a minute to listen for what the Spirit is saying in these verses...

COMMENT AND CONSIDER
In biblical times people lived with their extended families in homes made up of several rooms built around a central courtyard. In this courtyard several nuclear families shared life together, ate common meals, and carried out a family business. Jesus, along with his parents, brothers, and sisters, would have grown up in this kind of an extended family home. Their family business was construction, and Jesus himself was trained as a builder (Greek: *tekton*, see Mark 6:3). This word is often translated "carpenter," which in western culture evokes the image of a woodworker, but nearly all construction in ancient Israel was carried out with stone.

In these verses Jesus' background as a *tekton* comes through loud and clear. Jesus knew from experience that laying the stone walls of a house on the sandy alluvial soil common to that region was a recipe for disaster. Instead, a wise *tekton* would dig down to the basalt bedrock and lay the stones of a wall directly on this strong foundation. It is fascinating that the very house in which Jesus most likely grew up has recently come to light in Nazareth, and it is built directly on the sloping bedrock. In fact, one of the doors of that extended family home is carved right out of the bedrock itself!

Jesus is giving us a clear picture of the relationship between hearing God's word and doing God's word. The Pharisees were experts in the Law who taught its finer points and added their own rules on top of it. But they often failed to follow the true intent of the Law. Jesus said this is as foolish as laying the stones of your walls on shifting sand that will soon be washed away. Instead, Jesus shows us the direct connection between hearing and doing God's word in the Kingdom. Those who hear the revelation of God and then respond to that revelation by taking a concrete step of faith are building a house that will stand the test of time.

People were *"astonished"* at Jesus' teaching, not only because of the profound insights he conveyed, but also because he demonstrated by his actions the very truths he described with his words. This produced a powerful moral authority which was in stark contrast to the *"scribes"* (another word for trained rabbinical teachers) who so often didn't walk their talk. It is no accident that Matthew moves from these profound teachings of Jesus on the mountain directly into a description of his powerful miracles and moving acts of compassion. Matthew wants us to see that Jesus was modeling the life of both hearing and doing the word of God.

The Apostle Paul tells us, *"So faith comes from what is heard, and what is heard comes through the message about Christ."* (Romans 10:17) Here we see how doing is meant to flow from hearing. As we listen for the word of Jesus, faith is planted in our hearts. We are then called to exercise that faith by taking a concrete step. This is how we follow Jesus one step at a time. The wise builder listens for the word of Jesus and then exercises the faith that word produces by taking a step in the footsteps of Jesus. It is daily revelation and response. Are you listening for Jesus' word to you today? Are you exercising that faith with a concrete step? Are you building your house on the rock?

Reflect and Respond

What is Jesus saying to me right now?

What step of faith is Jesus calling me to take today?

DAY 17

READ AND LISTEN: MATTHEW 8:5-22
Take a minute to listen for what the Spirit is saying in these verses...

COMMENT AND CONSIDER
Capernaum was a medium-sized town on the north shore of the Sea of Galilee, renowned for its fishing. The famous trade route between Egypt and Damascus, known as the Via Maris ("the way of the sea"), curved around the lake and passed directly by Capernaum. Just to the east of Capernaum was the border between the regions ruled by Herod Antipas (Galilee) and his brother Herod Philip (Gaulanitis). Since this trade route and the border between these territories were both strategically important, the Romans stationed a detachment of soldiers outside of Capernaum. Archaeologists have confirmed this through the discovery of their camp.

A centurion was a professional officer of the Roman army who commanded 100 soldiers. Centurions carried considerable social status and power and were paid about 15 times as much as a common soldier. This centurion had a slave who was suffering from a painful paralysis that some have suggested may have been a form of polio, which was widespread in the ancient world. At his wits end, this centurion decided to approach Jesus for help.

The Jewish people generally hated the Romans as pagan conquerors and particularly despised the soldiers who enforced the collection of exorbitant taxes by traitorous tax collectors. Roman soldiers often harassed and sometimes abused the local people. So, it is unusual that this centurion would approach a Jewish rabbi for help.

But this was not your typical centurion. As Luke explains, the Jewish religious leaders told Jesus, *"he loves our nation and has built us a synagogue."* (Luke 7:5) This means the centurion is probably one of the many "God-fearers" in the Roman world. God-fearers were Gentiles that had come to believe in the God of the Jews but had not fully converted to Judaism by submitting to circumcision and all the ceremonial laws.

This God-fearing centurion demonstrated respect for Jewish sensibilities when he said, *"I am not worthy to have you come under my roof,"* knowing that Jews would consider a Roman home ritually unclean. Even more he demonstrated extraordinary faith in Jesus' authority when he professed his belief that Jesus could heal his slave, even from a distance. Usually, we hear people are amazed by Jesus, but this time it is Jesus who is amazed by a Roman military leader!

Jesus scandalously said, *"Truly I tell you, I have not found anyone in Israel with so great a faith."* He went on to say that when God's Kingdom has fully come, people from every background, including this hardened Gentile soldier, will be seated around the heavenly banquet table with the great heroes of the Bible, while members of the people of Israel are thrown into the outer darkness. This would have been considered a heretical statement by the religious establishment and a traitorous statement by the nationalistic rebels. But it was hard to argue with Jesus when he did exactly what the centurion believed he would… healed the slave from a distance!

It is so easy to put God in a box and draw lines of division around people based on our assumptions and prejudices. But God loves to work in the most surprising ways, and faith often comes from the places we least expect it. Who have you assumed is beyond the reach of God's grace and goodness? Who have you labeled as outside the sphere of God's reign? How might God be calling you to open yourself to them as Jesus did to this centurion?

Reflect and Respond
What is Jesus saying to me right now?

What step of faith is Jesus calling me to take today?

DAY 18

READ AND LISTEN: MATTHEW 8:23-34
Take a minute to listen for what the Spirit is saying in these verses…

COMMENT AND CONSIDER

About 35 years ago, a first-century fishing boat was discovered at the Sea of Galilee. It measures 28 feet long, 8 feet wide, had a removeable mast, and had places for four oars and a steering oar. It has been painstakingly restored, and now we can see the very type of boat that Jesus and his fishing disciples used during their mission around the lake.

Matthew tells us they were sailing across the lake *"to the other side,"* which means they were heading to the primarily Gentile eastern side of the Sea of Galilee. Although a large storm was brewing, Jesus fell asleep *"in the stern, sleeping on the cushion."* (Mark 4:38) It is common for the wind from the east to blow hot air off the desert highlands onto the cool air rising off the water, resulting in dramatic storms which can produce waves up to seven feet high on the lake.

As the storm pummeled the fishing boat, it began taking on water, but Jesus continued slumbering in peace. It was a powerful demonstration of both the weariness of his frail humanity and the profound trust in God with which he lived his life, whether waking or sleeping! Meanwhile, Jesus' disciples were absolutely freaking out, even though one-third of them were professional fishermen who had sailed this lake their entire life. When they finally woke Jesus up, he challenged them to a new level of trust in God by saying, *"Why are you afraid, you of little faith?"* Then Jesus proceeded to rebuke the wind and the sea, and suddenly a perfect calm overtook them.

It is good to remember that they were sailing to the Gentile side of the lake and Jesus was about to take on the legion of demons who had enslaved the Gadarene demoniac. The storm they encountered was a vivid picture of the spiritual battle into which they were entering. The sleepy Jesus who defeats the storm models for us what it means to live by faith in the Father in all circumstances, whether on glassy seas or in the midst of terrifying gales.

In Jesus' weariness we are reminded that Jesus was operating in his full humanity during his earthly mission, and yet he was a conduit for the supernatural power needed to do God's will. Jesus temporarily set aside his divinity for those thirty or so years so he could show us how to live as human beings filled with the Spirit and walking by faith. (See Philippians 2:6-7.) Jesus' disciples learned how to operate in the authority they had been given as daughters and sons of their Father the King, so they could follow the example of Jesus, even in his supernatural acts of prophecy, healing, and deliverance. I think Jesus was a little annoyed that they had not simply calmed the storm themselves without having to wake him up!

When you are facing the overwhelming storms of life, it is always good to cry out to Jesus. It is even better to follow Jesus' example of trusting the Father and exercising the authority given to us as sons and daughters of the King to fight the spiritual battles before us. What storms are you facing? How are you sleeping in the midst of them? What does it mean for you to confront those storms with the authority you have been given?

REFLECT AND RESPOND
What is God saying to me right now?

What step of faith is God calling me to take today?

Footsteps Every Week: Review

Write a brief summary of what Jesus said to you each day this past week and the step of faith he called you to take:

Monday

Tuesday

Wednesday

Thursday

Friday

Saturday

Footsteps Every Week: Reflect

Big Picture
As you look over what Jesus has said to you this past week, do you see any themes? What is the most important thing you need to remember and believe?

Predictable Pattern
As you look over what Jesus called you to do this past week, is there a new predictable pattern he is inviting you to establish in your life with God and others?

Plant the Word
As you look over the readings from this past week, write out the passage that feels most important for you and memorize it over the next week:

DAY 19

READ AND LISTEN: MATTHEW 9:1-13
Take a minute to listen for what the Spirit is saying in these verses…

COMMENT AND CONSIDER
Jesus returned from the east side of the lake to Capernaum, which Matthew describes as *"his own town."* Jesus is no longer a visitor in the extended family home of Simon and Andrew but has become part of the family (Greek: *oikos*), and their house has become the base of his mission. (See Matthew 12:47-50.) It was in this home that the paralytic was brought to Jesus.

Jesus' decision to address this man's spiritual brokenness before healing his physical ailment is a reminder that physical healing points to the deeper work of redemption and restoration that Jesus came to accomplish. Though the religious leaders who were present said nothing, inwardly they were outraged that Jesus would presume to forgive sins! Jesus had prophetic insight into their judgmental thoughts, and so he demonstrated his authority to forgive sins by healing this man. It is hard to argue with a paralyzed man walking!

If this gracious act of forgiveness were not offensive enough to the religious leaders, Jesus went on to do one of the most scandalous things of his entire life. He walked up to the tax office of Matthew (Hebrew name: Levi) and gave him the simple but powerful invitation, *"Follow me."* Since Capernaum was on a major trade route and near the border with another province, it makes sense that the Romans set up a tax office there to collect taxes from the merchants moving their goods along the road.

Tax collectors were the most hated members of the Jewish community because they were colluding with the enemy by collecting taxes for the Romans and making themselves rich by extorting the people for even higher payments. Disciples, on the other hand, were some of the most respected members of society. They had to apply to be accepted by a rabbi. Those accepted were the elite students who had passed the rabbi's many moral and academic standards.

Matthew was literally the last person anyone would have expected to become a disciple! Matthew himself would never have dreamed of applying to become a disciple. Then Jesus added to the scandal by going to Matthew's home, enjoying the rest of the day with his extended family and eating a meal with his morally questionable tax collector friends! Entering someone's home was a public act of affirmation and eating at their table was a covenantal act of friendship. When the religious leaders confronted Jesus about this scandal, he explained what it means to be salt and light when he said, *"It is not those who are well who need a doctor, but those who are sick."*

When Jesus looked Matthew in the eye and said, *"Follow me,"* he was unmistakably demonstrating that the Kingdom of heaven is ruled by grace. He was demonstrating that each of us is called to become a disciple of Jesus, without exception! When he entered Matthew's home and reclined at his table, he was showing us our mission is to demonstrate that everyone has a place in God's family.

Do you ever feel paralyzed in your sin and brokenness? Do you feel unworthy to be a disciple of Jesus? Jesus looks into your eyes today and says, "Daughter, your sins are forgiven." Jesus walks up to your tax booth today and says, "Follow me." Do you know anyone who feels paralyzed and unworthy? Jesus is calling you to recline at their table and show them the Kingdom of God.

Reflect and Respond
What is Jesus saying to me right now?

What step of faith is Jesus calling me to take today?

DAY 20

READ AND LISTEN: MATTHEW 9:14-26
Take a minute to listen for what the Spirit is saying in these verses...

COMMENT AND CONSIDER
Jesus demonstrated a deep continuity with God's revelation in the past. He often quoted from the Hebrew Scriptures and taught that *"not the smallest letter or one stroke of a letter will pass away from the law until all things are accomplished."* (Matthew 5:18) At the same time Jesus constituted a radical new revelation that challenged most of the standard religious interpretations of God's revelation from the past. Jesus fulfilled Isaiah's prophecy, *"Look, I am about to do something new; even now it is coming. Do you not see it?"* (Isaiah 43:19) In his Revelation to John, Jesus said, *"Look, I am making everything new."* (Revelation 21:5)

Jesus was the fulfillment of centuries of messianic prophecy and promises, but he was not the kind of Messiah people were expecting. The surprising nature of Jesus' words and actions excited the crowds and upset their leaders. It excited the crowds because it showed them God cares about their struggles and oppression and was prepared to do something about it through Jesus. It upset their leaders because it precipitated a change that threatened their position and power.

In the ancient world, wine was often carried in a leather bag that could stretch as the wine fermented and expanded. You would never put new, unfermented wine in an old stretched-out wineskin because it couldn't accommodate the expansion of the new wine and would simply burst as the wine fermented. Jesus said the new revelation he was bringing was like new wine and, as such, it needed fresh, flexible wineskins to contain it without bursting. Following the radical new way of life Jesus modeled for his disciples is the new wineskin that conveys the Good News of the Kingdom to the world.

A hemorrhaging woman was considered continually unclean by the religious leaders and therefore cut off from family and friends. This woman believed Jesus could heal her but assumed she could never get close enough to him due to her condition. So, she exercised incredible courage and faith to try and secretly touch the edge of Jesus' robe. The religious leaders would have considered this a terrible sin because she was making a rabbi ceremonially unclean.

When her shocking deed was brought to light before the crowd, everyone expected Jesus to condemn this wretched woman. That was the old wineskin. Instead, he affirmed her as a member of God's family and extolled her faith. That is the new wineskin! When Jesus arrived at the home of the synagogue leader, Jairus (see Luke 8:41), everyone expected him to join those mourning for his daughter who had just died. That was the old wineskin. Instead, Jesus raised his daughter from the dead. That is the new wineskin!

Jesus is offering you new wine today. Will you receive it as the hemorrhaging woman and Jairus did? Even more, he is sending you to offer this same gift to those you meet today. Will you be a new wineskin that can stretch and accommodate the surprising grace and startling power of the Good News of the Kingdom?

Reflect and Respond
What is Jesus saying to me right now?

What step of faith is Jesus calling me to take today?

DAY 21

READ AND LISTEN: MATTHEW 9:27-38
Take a minute to listen for what the Spirit is saying in these verses...

COMMENT AND CONSIDER
David was the unlikely shepherd boy who was anointed by Samuel to become king of Israel. His 23rd Psalm is one of the most-loved passages in the Bible because it so beautifully describes God as the ultimate Shepherd, a role David knew well. The two blind men who cried out to Jesus recognized him as the Son of David, a title pointing to the many Old Testament prophecies that the "anointed one" (Hebrew: *messiah*, Greek: *Christ*) would be a descendant of David. This Son of David is the ultimate King who will finally establish God's rule over the people of the world and all of creation itself.

When Jesus told his disciples that he was the Good Shepherd (see John 10:11), he was clearly pointing to his fulfillment of these Davidic promises and to Psalm 23, demonstrating that he is the ultimate anointed Shepherd King who has come to gather God's sheep and establish God's rule over all creation. When Jesus opened the eyes of the blind men, he was acting as the Shepherd King gathering his lost sheep. When Jesus delivered the mute man from demonization, he was acting as the anointed Shepherd King, binding up the wounds of his beloved sheep. When he saw the distressed and dejected crowds, he felt compassion for them because he saw their desperate need for a Good Shepherd.

When we recognize Jesus as the Messiah or attribute to him the title Christ, we are seeing what the blind men saw. We are recognizing Jesus as the Son of David who fulfills all the promises of God to anoint a Shepherd King to gather his lost sheep, care for them, and establish a Kingdom of justice and peace where they can thrive. What is different about this Shepherd King is that he does not make his sheep dependent upon him, but rather raises them up, trains them, and empowers them to become shepherds as well!

Discipleship is very much like shepherding. We learn to follow where our shepherd leads us, do what he tells us to do, and become more productive under his leadership. However, in God's Kingdom, sheep grow up to become shepherds. When Jesus looks at the crowd in need of a shepherd, he knows that in the limitations of his humanity he cannot shepherd each of these people himself, so he tells his disciples that they are going to learn how to become shepherds who care for the sheep. To use another metaphor, Jesus tells them they will become workers trained to bring in the harvest.

We like to say that every Jesus-shaped disciple looks like a sheep from the front, because they are following someone who is helping them follow Jesus. But they also look like a shepherd from the back, because they are inviting others to follow them as they follow Jesus. Jesus is the Good Shepherd who has compassion on the sheep who are without a shepherd. He gathers these sheep into his flock and cares for them through disciples who are learning how to shepherd his sheep. And those disciples are tasked with training and empowering these sheep to become shepherds who do the same.

In what way are you relating to Jesus as your Good Shepherd King? Who is the person or people in your life who are acting as shepherds to help you follow Jesus? Who are you inviting to follow you as you follow Jesus?

Reflect and Respond

What is Jesus saying to me right now?

What step of faith is Jesus calling me to take today?

DAY 22

READ AND LISTEN: MATTHEW 10:1-15
Take a minute to listen for what the Spirit is saying in these verses…

COMMENT AND CONSIDER
Disciples are called to follow. Apostles are sent out on mission. Jesus called people to both. He trained and empowered his disciples to become apostles, and he wants to do the same for us. Jesus trained his disciples by telling them about God's Kingdom and modeling a new way of life for them to imitate. When he sent them out on mission, he explicitly passed on to them the authority they needed to follow the example he was setting for them.

Authority is the right to represent someone and act on their behalf. Jesus claimed the authority given to him as the Son of his Father the King, and that was how he overcame the devil and carried out his mission. Jesus offers that same authority to those who will submit to him by faith, claim their identity as daughters and sons of God, and follow his example. When we exercise this authority, the power of God flows through us in the person of the Holy Spirit, who enables us to do God's will.

Jesus trained his disciples for mission using the following principles:

- Verse 5-6: Be clear on your missional focus: Jesus loved and welcomed all people, but he focused on the "lost sheep of the house of Israel," the Jewish peasants who lived in the small towns and villages of Galilee.
- Verse 7: Make the Kingdom of Heaven your central message. Jesus taught many different things, but they all pointed back to the new reality of God's reign that he was inviting people to participate in.
- Verse 8: Demonstrate the coming Kingdom by allowing the power of the Spirit to flow through you to touch others and do the will of God on earth as it is done in heaven.

- Verse 9-10: Don't focus on money or rely on your own resources, but trust God to provide. Jesus didn't have an income stream, a house, or an official title, but by faith he simply did what he saw the Father doing.
- Verse 11: Focus on investing in relationships with people who are receptive. Jesus offered his friendship widely and then invested in the people who reciprocated that friendship.
- Verse 12-13: Build a sense of extended family ("household" = *oikos*) with those people who are open to you. Jesus spent a lot of time in the extended family homes of the people who were open to him and eventually called them his own family.
- Verse 14: Don't get tangled up with people who are not responsive but move on to others who are. Jesus didn't invest time with those who resisted him. He spent his time with people who received him and responded to what he said and did.

If you are a disciple, you are also called to be an apostle. If you are following Jesus, he is also sending you on mission. Who are the lost sheep on whom Jesus is calling you to focus? How is he calling you to trust him in your mission? Can you articulate Jesus' Good News of the Kingdom? Are you learning to demonstrate that Kingdom by the power of the Spirit? Who is receptive and responsive to you? How are you investing in them? What does it mean to build a sense of extended family with them? From whom do you need to let go and move on

Reflect and Respond
What is Jesus saying to me right now?

What step of faith is Jesus calling me to take today?

DAY 23

READ AND LISTEN: MATTHEW 10:16-25

Take a minute to listen for what the Spirit is saying in these verses…

COMMENT AND CONSIDER

From one perspective it is difficult to imagine why anyone could have been opposed to Jesus and his message of love, humility, and service. Who can object to his countless compassionate acts of healing and deliverance, or even the practical miracles like feeding a multitude with five loaves and two fish or saving a boatful of disciples from a storm? And yet it is true that from the very beginning there was a persistent and even malevolent resistance to Jesus and his message.

When Jesus could barely walk, Herod the Great tried to wipe him from the face of the earth by killing all the baby boys in Bethlehem. When Jesus went home to Nazareth and announced the Messianic Age was about to begin for everyone, the townspeople tried to kill him while his own family refused to intervene. Once his message went public, the religious teachers accused him of heresy and blasphemy, even claiming he was demonized. By the time he raised Lazarus from the dead, the official leaders of Israel decided they would arrest and execute him. When they brought Jesus in chains to the Roman governor, Pilate condemned him to torture and death even though he knew Jesus was innocent.

Jesus was very clear with his disciples that his way was not the easiest or most comfortable way to live, but it was the most meaningful and fruitful by far. He showed his followers that, if they were going to follow him by living as part of God's coming Kingdom, it would bring them into direct conflict with the kingdoms of this world. Even more, it became clear these worldly powers were under the influence of the kingdom of darkness which is actively at war on this earth with the heavenly reign of God.

In this passage Jesus warns us that engaging in the mission of the Kingdom means coming into conflict with these dark and malevolent powers. Even members of our own families will sometimes oppose the Good News we bring and collude with these dark powers to destroy us. This warning is not meant to strike fear into our hearts, but rather to open our eyes and make us aware. Jesus is preparing us for the inevitable battles that lie ahead for all who follow him and seek his Kingdom.

Remarkably, Jesus does not tell us to arm ourselves to fight according to the way of the world. Instead, we are to enter this inhospitable mission field like sheep who are surrounded by wolves. If we are going to be Jesus' disciples, we will have to take up our cross. If we are going to follow Jesus' example, we will need to lay down our lives, both figuratively and, in some cases, literally as he did. Jesus' promise to us amid these wolves is that the Holy Spirit will guide and empower us to fulfill the mission no matter the cost. *"But when they hand you over, don't worry about how or what you are to speak. For you will be given what to say at that hour, because it isn't you speaking, but the Spirit of your Father is speaking through you."*

Have you counted the cost of following Jesus? How can you learn to rely on the Holy Spirit to overcome the challenges of the mission to which God has called you?

Reflect and Respond
What is Jesus saying to me right now?

What step of faith is Jesus calling me to take today?

DAY 24

READ AND LISTEN: MATTHEW 10:26-42
Take a minute to listen for what the Spirit is saying in these verses…

COMMENT AND CONSIDER
In this passage Jesus continues his warning about the cost of discipleship in a fallen and broken world where the kingdom of darkness is at work through the kingdoms of this world. He highlights the theme of division, even among those in our own families, over allegiance to different kingdoms. Because even our closest and most important relationships can be torn apart over this allegiance, Jesus calls us to put our love and commitment to him first, even above our immediate family members. No other Jewish rabbi ever called his disciples to love him more than their own parents. In this we see Jesus' claim to divinity, since only God can rightly call us to this level of ultimate commitment!

But Jesus shifts the focus from warning to encouragement in this passage. Three times he repeats the imperative, *"don't be afraid."* The reason Jesus gives for us to find courage in the face of persecution is the surpassing greatness of God. The One we follow and serve, the One for whom we might be persecuted, is infinitely more powerful and just than any enemy we can face in this life. And he knows every hair on our head. He knows when a sparrow falls and is so much more concerned about our well-being. He is all powerful and all loving and is always with us and for us.

For this reason, we don't need to be afraid, and we don't need to hide. In fact, Jesus says we should shout our testimony from the rooftops regardless of the consequences, because in the end the truth will be vindicated and all that is true will be fully revealed. Jesus promises that if we openly acknowledge our relationship with him, he will in turn represent us before the Father. If we choose to deny him in the face of persecution, he in turn will deny us before the Father. Jesus is showing us how important it is to see the big picture when we are under pressure to deny our faith. He is helping us understand that faithfulness to him is worth more than anything this world can offer or take away.

Jesus does offer his followers peace (see John 14:27), but that peace is not the absence of strife. The peace Jesus offers comes to us amid inevitable conflict. He also offers the promise of special reward for those who come alongside the persecuted and offer welcome and support, even as simple as a cup of cold water.

Jesus is crystal clear: to follow him is to take up our own cross. While nearly all of Jesus' core group of disciples were killed for their testimony, and today many around the world still face the same fate, most of us in the western world face much more subtle pressures to deny our faith. Persecution may come as a cutting comment or a joke at our expense. It may be a social snub or a lost friendship. It may come as a delayed promotion or a withheld business deal. But these are pressures none the less. How do you respond to even the subtle cost of following Jesus in your context? How can you overcome the fear that might keep you from sharing your testimony of faith with someone? What does it mean to acknowledge Jesus before others even if it is not always popular?

REFLECT AND RESPOND

What is Jesus saying to me right now?

What step of faith is Jesus calling me to take today?

Footsteps Every Week: Review

Write a brief summary of what Jesus said to you each day this past week and the step of faith he called you to take:

Monday

Tuesday

Wednesday

Thursday

Friday

Saturday

Footsteps Every Week: Reflect

Big Picture

As you look over what Jesus has said to you this past week, do you see any themes? What is the most important thing you need to remember and believe?

Predictable Pattern

As you look over what Jesus called you to do this past week, is there a new predictable pattern he is inviting you to establish in your life with God and others?

Plant the Word

As you look over the readings from this past week, write out the passage that feels most important for you and memorize it over the next week:

DAY 25

READ AND LISTEN: MATTHEW 11:1-15
Take a minute to listen for what the Spirit is saying in these verses…

COMMENT AND CONSIDER
Jesus' relative John had prepared the way for his coming by preaching in the desert and baptizing in the Jordan River. John was very clear that he himself was not the Messiah and that the Messiah was far more important than he was. He also used fiery language to describe the Messiah's mission. John said of the Messiah, *"He himself will baptize you with the Holy Spirit and fire. His winnowing shovel is in his hand, and he will clear his threshing floor and gather his wheat into the barn. But the chaff he will burn with fire that never goes out."* (Matthew 3:11-12)

Jesus quoted Isaiah 61 to describe his mission, *"The Spirit of the Lord is on me, because he has anointed me to preach good news to the poor. He has sent me to proclaim release to the captives and recovery of sight to the blind, to set free the oppressed, to proclaim the year of the Lord's favor."* (Luke 4:18-19)

By this time John had been imprisoned by Herod Antipas, ruler of Galilee, in the formidable stone fortress called Machaerus overlooking the eastern shore of the Dead Sea. John had seen Jesus anointed by the Spirit in the Jordan River. Now, as John sat in Herod's dungeon, he was receiving reports from his disciples that Jesus was giving sight to the blind, delivering those oppressed by demons, and preaching Good News to the peasants of Galilee. It sounded as if Jesus was fulfilling Isaiah's prophecy in very Messianic fashion! And yet, Jesus had still not released John from his captivity.

Most Jews in the first century assumed the coming Messiah would be a conquering king who would overthrow the Romans, boot out the Herodians, and establish an independent Jewish kingdom like the one David established. When John sent his disciples to ask Jesus if he really was the Messiah, there was a kind of unspoken message: "If you really are the Messiah, why haven't you sprung me from prison yet?" Maybe John thought Jesus had forgotten about him and just needed a little reminder.

Jesus' response made it clear he was fulfilling Isaiah's messianic prophecy, but not in the way John might assume. He was healing, and delivering, and proclaiming Good News, but he was not establishing an earthly kingdom through military might. Jesus' messianic plan didn't include rescuing John. This must have been hard for John to hear, but it was an important corrective for all those who followed Jesus. They needed to understand that he was going to rule, not by overthrowing a political regime, but by laying down his life in self-giving sacrifice. John was learning what it meant to take up his cross and follow Jesus on this path of sacrificial love.

Although Jesus didn't offer a prison break, he did affirm the incredible importance of John in God's plan. He even lifted up John as the fulfillment of the prophecy in Malachi that Elijah would return to prepare the way for the coming of the Messiah. (Malachi 3:1; 4:5) However, he pointed out that the Kingdom of Heaven is going to face opposition and even violence for those who choose to follow him. John was the first one called to lay down his life for the sake of the Kingdom. How does it affect your faith to know that Jesus does not necessarily rescue his followers from suffering and even violence? What sacrifices may Jesus not rescue you from even if you ask him?

REFLECT AND RESPOND
What is Jesus saying to me right now?

What step of faith is Jesus calling me to take today?

DAY 26

READ AND LISTEN: MATTHEW 11:16-24

Take a minute to listen for what the Spirit is saying in these verses…

COMMENT AND CONSIDER

It is hard to imagine anyone ignoring Jesus' revolutionary call to a new life of transforming love and community, especially when we consider the authority of his teaching style and the confirming power of his miracles, but many did. It is tempting to assume Jesus' ministry was one glorious success story after another, but that is not the case. Although Jesus drew huge crowds to hear him teach and witness his miracles, most of them were fickle consumers who did not really embrace his vision of the Kingdom or commit to following him and joining in his mission. When this fickle consumerism became apparent, John describes how Jesus raised the bar of challenge in his teaching until most of the crowds went away. (See John 6:22-71.)

In biblical times children played a game called "wedding" in which they mimicked the joyous music and dancing that accompanied a marriage celebration. Another game was "funeral" in which they mimicked the procession of mourners walking to the cemetery while singing a dirge. In verses 16-17 Jesus likens these fickle consumers, who were unwilling to commit to a lifestyle of discipleship and mission, to children on the street who refused to join in these musical games.

Some people will criticize you and resist your message no matter what you say or do. The same people who questioned John's sanity for his abstinence judged Jesus as morally compromised for his consumption. Jesus points out the futility of living for the approval of others. He was crystal clear that his focus was on pleasing the Father and doing what he saw the Father doing, regardless of how others responded. (See John 5:19.) However, Jesus did not want a single stray sheep to be lost. He was also not afraid to call people out for their stubborn resistance to being found.

There were three Jewish towns on the northern shore of the Sea of Galilee where Jesus is reported to have invested most of his time and energy: Capernaum, Chorazin, and Bethsaida. For this reason, some have called the area encompassed by these three towns "the Evangelical Triangle." Despite the crowds he drew from these towns, relatively few ended up actually following Jesus. Because of this Jesus speaks a harsh word of judgment over them, saying that the residents of the most infamous pagan cities would have repented much sooner if they had heard his teaching and witnessed the same miracles.

The biblical word for repentance (Greek: *metanoia*) is more than just feeling regret over our sins. It literally means a change of mind, describing the new perspective that comes from listening to God's voice. Jesus' call to *"repent and believe"* is an invitation to hear his voice and take a step of faith in response to that word. It is what these daily devotions are all about! And yet this passage is a reminder that not everyone listens to the voice of Jesus. And even those who do often fail to respond by exercising the faith his word creates. (See Romans 10:17.)

Do you ever feel like a kid who is playing the wedding game, but the other kids aren't joining in? So did Jesus. Do you ever feel like some of the people in whom you have invested the most time and energy are the least responsive? So did Jesus. I am so glad Jesus didn't let those disappointments stop him from pressing on and completing his mission! And what about you? Can you hear the music Jesus is playing? Are you joining him in the dance? Are you repenting and believing today?

Reflect and Respond
What is Jesus saying to me right now?

What step of faith is Jesus calling me to take today?

DAY 27

READ AND LISTEN: MATTHEW 11:25-28
Take a minute to listen for what the Spirit is saying in these verses...

COMMENT AND CONSIDER
People in the biblical world were familiar with the wooden yoke that bound two oxen together to allow them to pull farm implements or a cart loaded with cargo. The rabbis used this as a metaphor for their teaching and pictured their students taking up the yoke of the Law. One rabbi put it this way, "He that takes upon himself the yoke of the Law, from him shall be taken away the yoke of the worldly kingdom and the yoke of worldly care; but he that throws off the yoke of the Law, upon him shall be laid the yoke of the worldly kingdom and the yoke of worldly care." (m. 'Abot 3:5)

The Pharisees took enthusiasm for the yoke of the Law to a new level. They identified 613 written laws of the Old Testament and added to them innumerable binding interpretations of the tiniest detail which were not written down but passed on orally from one generation of rabbis to the next. This resulted in an incredibly complex web of legal requirements and religious practices which was very difficult for ordinary people to observe. Jesus said, *"They tie up heavy loads that are hard to carry and put them on people's shoulders..."* (Matthew 23:4)

Instead of promoting Law observance as the basis for our acceptance by God, Jesus freely accepted people as they were and proclaimed the Father's love as the basis for living according to his will. He taught that laborers who work different hours are paid the same amount. (Matthew 20:1-16) The prodigal son is embraced as enthusiastically as the older brother who stayed home. (Luke 15:11-32) Jesus welcomed tax collectors and prostitutes as friends and disciples.

Jesus did not compromise the biblical Law but actually intensified its moral imperative as the vision of the Kingdom. He did not try to motivate people to fulfill this vision through threats of punishment, but rather by a response to grace and love. As he said of the sinful woman who responded to Jesus by washing his feet with her tears, *"Therefore I tell you, her many sins have been forgiven; that's why she loved much. But the one who is forgiven little, loves little."* (Luke 7:47)

It is so easy to turn the vision of the Kingdom into a new set of religious obligations and legalistic rules, but as Peter said this is *"putting a yoke on the disciples' necks that neither our ancestors nor we have been able to bear."* (Acts 15:10) Paul said it this way: *"For freedom, Christ set us free. Stand firm, then, and don't submit again to a yoke of slavery."* (Galatians 5:1) Jesus came to set us free from the heavy yoke of religious legalism and from the destructive illusion that we don't need any yoke at all. Instead, he invites us into a close discipling relationship with him in which we take up his light and easy yoke. This is where our soul finally finds true rest and we can begin to bear good fruit that lasts.

I love Eugene Peterson's version of this passage from The Message: *"Are you tired? Worn out? Burned out on religion? Come to me. Get away with me and you'll recover your life. I'll show you how to take a real rest. Walk with me and work with me—watch how I do it. Learn the unforced rhythms of grace. I won't lay anything heavy or ill-fitting on you. Keep company with me and you'll learn to live freely and lightly."* Which yoke are you carrying today?

Reflect and Respond
What is Jesus saying to me right now?

What step of faith is Jesus calling me to take today?

DAY 28

READ AND LISTEN: MATTHEW 12:1-21
Take a minute to listen for what the Spirit is saying in these verses…

COMMENT AND CONSIDER

The Jewish people were the only nation in the ancient world who observed a day of rest each week. It was an incredible gift to have an entire 24-hour period in which no work was done and people were set free to rest, recreate, and be renewed. However, somewhere along the way the purpose of this gift got lost. The religious teachers tried to guard the gift by adding many rules to it. Eventually the gift became a burden, and it was very difficult to observe the Sabbath according to the regulations enforced by the Pharisees.

Jesus cut through the accumulation of human rules and religious traditions that obscured God's good intent in his Covenant with the people of Israel. He was particularly determined to return the gift of Sabbath to God's children. He grew up observing the Sabbath and continued to teach his disciples to do so, but he emphasized the purpose of the gift: to be a blessing of rest and renewal. Jesus was severely criticized by the Pharisees because he did not observe the many rules they added to the Sabbath. Jesus wanted to be clear that the Sabbath was created for the sake of people, not the other way around!

Jesus emphasized that the written Scriptures superseded any of the interpretations the Pharisees turned into new religious rules. For instance, when the Pharisees accused Jesus' disciples of breaking the Sabbath because they were gleaning from the field in order to eat, Jesus responded by pointing out the biblical precedent set by David and Ahimelech when he was given the offering bread from the temple in Nob to eat. (See 1 Samuel 21:1-6.)

Further, Jesus pointed out that the priests in the Temple have to work on the Sabbath in order to keep the sacrificial system functioning. (See Numbers 28:9-10; 1 Chronicles 9:32.) The rabbis had a rule of interpretation called *qal wahomer* (Hebrew for "light and heavy") which said if something was true in a less important situation, it was certainly true in a more important context. Jesus asserted that he and the Kingdom he is proclaiming are *"greater than the temple."* Based on this Jesus uses the *qal wahomer* principle to point out that if the priests can do God's will on the Sabbath, so can he and his disciples because their mission is even more important.

Jesus pointed out that some rabbis allowed for the saving of an endangered animal on the Sabbath. Applying the same rabbinical principle, since caring for a human being is more important than an animal, Jesus often chose to heal on the Sabbath. One of Jesus' primary principles was to simply do on earth what he saw the Father in heaven doing. (See John 5:19.) He was not afraid to do something good that he sensed the Father was doing on the Sabbath, even if some people might classify it as "work." Matthew reports that the Pharisees began plotting how to murder him, not just because they believed he was breaking the Sabbath, but because he claimed to be greater than the Temple and proclaimed himself *"Lord of the Sabbath."*

Do you have an intentional plan to observe a weekly 24-hour Sabbath rest in which you don't do any unnecessary work? If not, why not? If so, how can you make sure you are receiving the gift of rest and renewal your Father wants to give you?

Reflect and Respond
What is the Spirit saying to me right now?

What step of faith is the Spirit calling me to take today?

DAY 29

READ AND LISTEN: MATTHEW 12:22-32
Take a minute to listen for what God is saying in these verses…

COMMENT AND CONSIDER
It is striking to realize how much time Jesus spent healing people from physical brokenness and delivering people from spiritual bondage. Both were an aspect of the salvation Jesus offered, and both were an expression of his love and compassion for the hurting. (See Matthew 9:22; 14:14.) In a broken world trapped under the power of darkness, it was inevitable that Jesus' demonstration of God's Kingdom would come up against strong demonic opposition. Often demonic forces work through people in unseen ways, but Jesus' very presence seemed to provoke demons to reveal themselves. They usually addressed Jesus directly, recognizing his divine authority, even begging him for mercy. (See Matthew 8:29-31.)

First-century exorcists used complex incantations and esoteric rituals to try and drive out demons. The Jewish historian Josephus tells of an exorcist named Eleazar who used a signet ring and a root to dramatically pull a demon out of a man's nose. Another Jewish exorcist used fish livers and hearts. Jesus used none of these sensationalist techniques, but directly addressed the demons in the authority given to him by his Father the King and ordered them to leave. And they left! In verse 28 Jesus pointed out that his ability to cast out demons by the power of the Spirit was an unmistakable sign that the Kingdom of God was breaking into the kingdoms of this world.

The religious leaders were profoundly threatened by all this and tried to deny that Jesus' authority and power came from God. Instead, they came up with the explanation that Jesus was actually using demonic power to drive out demons. This accusation was maintained for centuries among Jewish leaders who described Jesus as a "sorcerer." Jesus responded by pointing out the logical absurdity of demons driving out demons. Instead, Jesus pointed out that to rescue a person from bondage to a demon, you must first subdue the demon to *"plunder his house."*

Jesus highlights the seriousness of this accusation that he is operating in demonic power rather than the power of the Spirit by warning them that the only unforgivable sin is *"blasphemy against the Spirit."* Jesus is able to forgive all our sins no matter how wicked, but he will not force his grace upon us if we are unwilling to accept him. In the end, if we refuse to accept the Holy Spirit's witness to the truth of Jesus as our Savior and Lord, we will be rejecting the gift of his saving grace. This is the only unforgivable sin.

It would be easy to assume that Jesus was able to bind demons and rescue the demonized because he is God, but Jesus made it clear that his power came from the Holy Spirit working through him. He also made it clear that he was passing on the authority given to him as the Son of God to the daughters and sons of God who are part of his new family and Kingdom. That is why his followers were able to go out and do all the things he did, including healing and casting out demons. (Matthew 10:1, 8) This means we have access to this same authority and power as God's sons and daughters.

Can you recognize any tendency inside of you to resist the work of the Holy Spirit? How can you let that resistance go and yield more control of your life to the Spirit? How can this lead you into greater confidence that you have received the authority to overcome the enemy of your soul?

REFLECT AND RESPOND
What is Jesus saying to me right now?

What step of faith is Jesus calling me to take today?

DAY 30

READ AND LISTEN: MATTHEW 12:33-45
Take a minute to listen for what God is saying in these verses...

COMMENT AND CONSIDER
When God first created the heavens and the earth, he declared it all good and declared human beings very good. God designed us for a close covenantal relationship with him and with each other. He also gave us a clear kingdom calling to represent him by ruling over creation and multiplying the goodness of his creation. (See Genesis 1:27-28.) Sadly, when Adam and Eve decided to take charge of their own lives and replace God, it threw his perfect design into chaos. This broken world with its sinful humanity is the bitter result.

But God refused to give up on us and has continually pursued our redemption by choosing the people of Israel and making a series of covenants, which culminated in the New Covenant Jesus established and the New Creation he inaugurated. Now, in the person of Jesus—in his life, teaching, death, and resurrection—we see how humanity and all of creation can be redeemed, restored, and renewed! This is what Matthew calls the Good News of the Kingdom.

As disciples of Jesus, we have been called to live in this New Covenant and follow him into this New Creation by imitating his way of life and allowing the Spirit to fill us and empower us to do God's will on earth as it is in heaven. We are being restored to our original calling to represent God and multiply the goodness of his creation.

Jesus tells us there are two kinds of people in this world: those who are trapped in the darkness of this broken creation and are expanding what is bad, and those who are being redeemed in the light of the New Creation and are expanding what is good. He uses the metaphor of good fruit and bad fruit to help us discern the difference between these two ways of life. If we are in relationship with Jesus through his New Covenant and are walking with him by faith, then we will become a good tree that naturally produces good fruit. If we are trying to live this life by our own strength or wisdom, we will inevitably become a bad tree that naturally produces bad fruit.

Jesus called the Pharisees a *"brood of vipers"* because, although they were religious leaders, they were not part of the New Covenant and Creation. They were trying to serve God and do good by their own wisdom and strength, so they couldn't help but produce bad fruit. A heart not submitted to God inevitably produces a storehouse full of bad fruit. A heart submitted to God inevitably produces a storehouse full of good fruit.

Jesus said repentance is the key to becoming a tree that produces good fruit and fills a storehouse with what is good. Repentance means listening to God and allowing his Word to change our mind and alter the direction of our life. The pagan queen Sheba and the Ninevites both repented and became good trees producing good fruit. It is not enough to remove the evil that is in us—otherwise more evil spirits can come and fill the vacuum. We need to be filled with the Holy Spirit who alone can drive out the evil inside of us and transform us into a good tree producing good fruit.

Are you a good tree or a bad tree? What does it mean for you to be rooted in Jesus and filled with his Spirit? How can you naturally start to fill your storehouse with good things?

Reflect and Respond
What is Jesus saying to me right now?

What step of faith is Jesus calling me to take today?

Footsteps Every Week: Review

Write a brief summary of what Jesus said to you each day this past week and the step of faith he called you to take:

Monday

Tuesday

Wednesday

Thursday

Friday

Saturday

Footsteps Every Week: Reflect

Big Picture
As you look over what Jesus has said to you this past week, do you see any themes? What is the most important thing you need to remember and believe?

Predictable Pattern
As you look over what Jesus called you to do this past week, is there a new predictable pattern he is inviting you to establish in your life with God and others?

Plant the Word
As you look over the readings from this past week, write out the passage that feels most important for you and memorize it over the next week:

DAY 31

READ AND LISTEN: MATTHEW 12:46-13:9
Take a minute to listen for what the Spirit is saying in these verses…

COMMENT AND CONSIDER

Jesus was teaching in Simon and Andrew's extended family home in Capernaum, and as usual the courtyard was filled with people. Jesus' family back in Nazareth heard reports of the things he was doing and concluded he had gone crazy! (See Mark 3:20-21.) Mary and his four brothers came looking for Jesus, presumably to take him back to Nazareth and nurse him back to mental health. (See Mark 3:31-32.) But when they arrived, so many people were in the courtyard of Simon and Andrew's home that they couldn't even enter through the outer door. So they asked to see Jesus. When this message was passed through the crowd to one of the rooms in the house Jesus responded in a very unexpected way.

In first-century Jewish culture, your identity was rooted primarily in your family. Honoring your father and mother was considered one of your highest moral obligations. When Jesus said, *"Who is my mother and who are my brothers?"* he was distancing of himself from his own family in a shocking way. Then Jesus looked at the disciples seated around him and said, *"Here are my mother and my brothers! For whoever does the will of my Father in heaven is my brother and sister and mother."* This was a revolutionary new vision of what a family can be.

Jesus was redefining family, not solely based on marriage and genetics, but based on our calling to represent God and do his will on earth as it is done in heaven. We will see in the next chapter that Jesus did go to his family and hometown of Nazareth, but both rejected his vision of the Kingdom. Jesus wasn't rejecting his biological family, but he also wasn't going to let them derail his mission. To use the image of his parable of the soils, he cast his seed on the soil of Nazareth and his extended family, but they were not good soil. Perhaps their hearts had been hardened by the oppression they endured. Perhaps the devil snatched the seed away before it could sink into their minds.

When Jesus sowed the seed of God's Word in Capernaum, he found good soil. He found people of peace who were receptive and responsive to his vision of the Kingdom. When Simon invited him into his extended family, Jesus knew this was now his new home and he showed them a whole new way to be a family. He taught them how to live as a family of disciples on mission together, living out the Good News of the Kingdom. And this soil produced good fruit: thirty, sixty, and a hundred times what was sown!

After Jesus' death and resurrection, when he commissioned this extended family to make disciples and take the Good News of the Kingdom to the ends of the earth, they continued to follow this same pattern of multiplying Jesus-shaped families of disciples who were living on mission together. It came to be called "the church." As he promised, Jesus built a church made up of extended spiritual families on mission who continued to follow his way and do the will of God. This is how the Kingdom comes still today!

How do you define your family? What is the role of God's will in your family? How could you build a family that looks more like Jesus' family on mission?

Reflect and Respond
What is Jesus saying to me right now?

What step of faith is Jesus calling me to take today?

DAY 32

READ AND LISTEN: MATTHEW 13:10-23
Take a minute to listen for what the Spirit is saying in these verses...

COMMENT AND CONSIDER
First-century Jewish culture was primarily an oral culture. Jewish boys from about five to twelve years old learned to read the Law in *Beth Sefer*, the weekday elementary school taught by the rabbis in the synagogue. But because written documents were so expensive, most people rarely had an opportunity to read outside of school. This is why stories were so important in that culture. Still today it is common for people in Jerusalem to sit on rooftops at night with friends sipping coffee and reciting epic poem and stories from memory, as I have often been privileged to do.

This is the reason Jesus told so many parables. Jesus' parables were short stories rooted in everyday experiences from real life that painted pictures of the Kingdom of God. Often listeners had to wrestle with these simple stories to discern the deeper meaning Jesus intended. This seems to be why the disciples ask Jesus about his parables. They had trouble understanding their meaning and wondered why Jesus didn't just speak more plainly to the crowds.

Jesus responded by saying that the parables reveal the *"secrets of the kingdom of heaven"* to some but conceal those *"secrets"* from others. Then he quoted Isaiah 6:9-10 to explain the diagnostic function of the parables. The parables are meant to reveal who is open to the Good News of the Kingdom and who is not. Those who are not open will *"listen, but never understand... look, but never perceive."* God is not hiding the meaning from them, but their hearts have become callous and ears have become hard of hearing and eyes are shut tight.

This parable of the soils is a picture of the very reason Jesus is giving for telling parables. Those who are hard, rocky, or thorny soil will not receive the message of the parable, or the devil will snatch it from them. Those who are good soil will receive the parable, its meaning will take root in them, and they will produce the good fruit of the Kingdom. The reason Jesus chose some very unlikely people to be his disciples is because they were the ones who had ears to hear and eyes to see the Kingdom Jesus' parables were revealing.

Jesus didn't explain the parables to the crowds, but to the disciples who were receptive and ready to respond. Typically, farmers would scatter seed across their fields ("broadcast sowing") as opposed to carefully placing them in furrows, and the seed would land on all kinds of soil. Since farming families lived in the village and walked out to work their fields each day, hard-packed paths surrounded the fields. Much of the topography of Israel is comprised of a thin layer of topsoil spread across limestone bedrock that can keep roots from going deep. Where there is soil, it is normal for weeds to grow up among the crops that are planted.

In all these familiar scenarios, we see Jesus' point: the Kingdom of Heaven is for those who will receive and respond to Jesus' word; those who are willing to repent and believe. What kind of soil are you? Is there some hardness that needs to be plowed up? Is there shallowness that needs to be deepened? Are there weeds that need to be pulled? Do you need to drive away some birds? Are you willing to wrestle with the truths of the Kingdom until they become real in your life?

Reflect and Respond

What is Jesus saying to me right now?

What step of faith is Jesus calling me to take today?

DAY 33

READ AND LISTEN: MATTHEW 13:24-35
Take a minute to listen for what the Spirit is saying in these verses…

COMMENT AND CONSIDER
We are a mixed bag, aren't we? To differing degrees, we are all still tangled up in sin and under the influence of darkness. When we have carefully plowed a field and sown seeds in the clean ground, we naively expect a field full of wheat at harvest time. But inevitably the end result is a mixture of good grain and invasive weeds. The wind blows the seeds of unwanted species into our field without us even being aware. Our enemies can intentionally try to sabotage our harvest by spreading noxious seeds among the good ones. The word translated *"weeds"* here denotes a kind of rye grass with poisonous seeds, which in early stages of growth looks a lot like wheat but can be distinguished easily in its mature state at the time of harvesting.

If you were a farmer and saw weeds popping up in your wheat field, it would be tempting to start pulling them immediately. But you might have trouble distinguishing wheat sprouts from weed sprouts. Also, the young wheat plants are so fragile that you might end up damaging them, compromising the harvest of good grain. Instead, Jesus tells us to wait until the harvest. Once the grain is on the stalk, then the good can be distinguished from the bad. Then the weeds can be effectively separated from the wheat. No matter how dedicated we are to producing a good harvest, sin will inevitably invade and take root in our soil.

The twelve full-time disciples were personally chosen and trained by Jesus, but one of them ended up selling Jesus out to the religious authorities for 30 pieces of silver. When we read Paul's letters to the first communities of disciples, we hear about the sin, pride, division, and false teaching that infiltrated these spiritual families. Even the very first church was a mixed bag!

If you are part of a church for more than about five minutes, you become painfully aware that you're in a community made up of both well-meaning people and those with false motives. If you stick around the church long enough, you will start to see there is an enemy at work trying to subvert the mission of the church by sowing bad seeds into the soil. But Jesus warns us that we will damage this spiritual community if we try to sort out the good from the bad too soon. It is too hard to tell them apart. It is better to wait until the fruit has proven the good from the bad. Ultimately, it is better to let the Lord of the harvest sort it all out in the end.

Matthew records two more parables, one of which shows us that, like a mustard seed, God often brings great things out of that which seems insignificant. The other reminds us that, like leaven in dough, God's Kingdom can secretly infiltrate the hearts of people, transforming their lives and impacting an entire community.

How do you deal with the mixed bag of broken human community? Are you tempted to slip into judging others, or are you willing to leave that up to God? Do you believe that, despite your own brokenness, God can bring great things out of your life even when you feel insignificant? How can you be part of the Kingdom leaven that is quietly transforming this broken world?

Reflect and Respond

What is Jesus saying to me right now?

What step of faith is Jesus calling me to take today?

DAY 34

READ AND LISTEN: MATTHEW 13:36-46
Take a minute to listen for what the Spirit is saying in these verses...

COMMENT AND CONSIDER
After explaining the parable of the weeds to his disciples, Jesus told them two more short stories that illustrate the relative value of seeking the Kingdom of God. The first is about a man who stumbles across a treasure chest buried in the ground. Although the Temple in Jerusalem functioned as a bank where people could deposit money for safekeeping, most people kept their savings in a strong box which they buried under the floor of a room in their house. Archaeologists often find hoards of coins buried in the floors of ancient buildings they excavate. A farming family that owned fields outside the village could hide a larger chest of valuables there as well.

The reason archaeologists sometimes find hoards of coins is that whoever buried them died before they could dig them up or tell others where they were. Jesus imagines such a scenario when he describes this man who discovered a treasure buried in a field. If those valuables were worth significantly more than the field itself and the owners of the field didn't know about the buried treasure, this was an opportunity to massively multiply his wealth. Obviously that man would do whatever he could to raise the money to buy the field because it was worth so much more than the purchase price.

The second story is about a merchant who was searching for the finest and most beautiful pearls. He was not simply interested in making money but was passionate about the aesthetic value of these jewels. When he discovered the most breath-taking pearl he had ever seen, he was so taken with it he sold all the other pearls in his collection to acquire this one unique and priceless pearl.

In both of these parables, Jesus gives us a picture of how much more valuable the Kingdom of God is than the things to which we normally ascribe value. In both stories the subject discovers something worth more than everything else they own. In chapter 19 Matthew records the time a rich young ruler came to Jesus for guidance, and Jesus called him to sell everything, give the proceeds to the poor, and come follow him. The man was shaken by this challenge and went away sad. Afterward Peter said to Jesus, *"See, we have left everything and followed you. So what will there be for us?"* Jesus replied, *"And everyone who has left houses or brothers or sisters or father or mother or children or fields because of my name will receive a hundred times more and will inherit eternal life."* (See Matthew 19:16-30.)

Jesus is helping us recognize that seeking the Kingdom of God is worth more than everything else in our lives combined. As he said in chapter 16, when we seek his Kingdom first, every other thing will be added. The rich young ruler didn't realize the Kingdom treasure was buried in his own proverbial field. If he did, he would have seen it was worth so much more than all his possessions. He didn't see he was being offered a priceless pearl. Jesus doesn't want us to make the same mistake.

Have you discovered the treasure of the Kingdom hidden in the field? The priceless pearl? What are you willing to give up to acquire that treasure? What is one thing you can give up that is keeping you from living more fully in the Kingdom of God today?

Reflect and Respond
What is Jesus saying to me right now?

What step of faith is Jesus calling me to take today?

DAY 35

READ AND LISTEN: MATTHEW 13:47-58

Take a minute to listen for what the Spirit is saying in these verses...

COMMENT AND CONSIDER

As we have seen, Jesus was deeply rooted in the Hebrew scriptures and intensified the demand of the Law. (See Matthew 5:17-48.) But at the same time, he offered new insights that challenged the religious status quo, amazed the people, and threatened their leaders. Jesus claimed to fulfill the ancient Messianic prophecies for which people had been waiting generations to be fulfilled (see Luke 4:18-21), yet at the same time his teaching of the Kingdom of Heaven was a fresh vision of God's will unfolding on earth. Jesus said his disciples would need to learn how to hold together both the ancient truths of scripture and the new reality manifesting before their very eyes in the person and mission of Jesus.

To describe this, Jesus drew on the image of a man who had buried his valuables in a strongbox underneath the floor in the storage room of his house. Disciples in the Kingdom of Heaven are those who know how to dig up the ancient treasures and add the new treasures Jesus offers, just as a homeowner adds new coins to the valuable heirlooms stored in the family strongbox.

When Jesus returned to his hometown of Nazareth and taught in their synagogue, this combination of old and new caused a stir. Matthew tells us Jesus' message in the synagogue that day both *"astonished"* and *"offended"* the people of Nazareth. Luke gives more detail about Jesus' sermon, explaining that he announced the dawning of the long-awaited Messianic Age but added the inclusion of the Gentiles in God's coming Kingdom. (See Luke 4:16-30.) The fulfillment of Messianic promises was the ancient treasure, but the new spin was that the Messiah was coming for everyone, even pagan Gentiles!

Matthew points out that not only the townspeople rejected Jesus' message of radical inclusion, but even his own *"household"* (Greek: *"oikos"*) couldn't accept his vision of the Kingdom. This must have been deeply painful for Jesus, and it is certainly why he went to Capernaum and built a new kind of extended family with Simon and Andrew and their *oikos*. But Jesus never rejected his family, even when they rejected him. It is encouraging to see that at least his mother Mary and his brothers James and Jude (and maybe the other brothers and sisters?) eventually embraced Jesus and his Messianic vision of the Kingdom of God. (See John 19:25-27; 1 Corinthians 15:7.)

Perhaps this is an example of Jesus' parables of the weeds in the field and the dragnet full of fish. Just as nets collected fish of different species, both those considered "clean" and "unclean" according to the ritual purity laws, so will the sharing of the Good News. We will always end up with a mixed bag of people who are with us and those who are not. Jesus is telling us not to reject them as he did not reject his family. Perhaps they will come around; let God sort it out in the end. But just as he left Nazareth and refused to return home when his family thought he was crazy (see Mark 3:20-35), so we must not allow those who don't understand the nature of God's Kingdom to draw us away from the path of following the footsteps of Jesus.

Are you a disciple who can bring forth treasures both old and new? What is your response to those who are not receptive to your message? Can you withhold judgment while refusing to allow anyone to draw you away from the path Jesus has set for you?

Reflect and Respond

What is Jesus saying to me right now?

What step of faith is Jesus calling me to take today?

DAY 36

READ AND LISTEN: MATTHEW 14:1-14
Take a minute to listen for what the Spirit is saying in these verses…

COMMENT AND CONSIDER
When Herod the Great died, his territory was divided between three of his many sons; Archelaus ruled over Judea in the south, Antipas ruled Galilee in the north, and Philip ruled Golan in the northeast. Each of the three also received the title Tetrarch. Another son of Herod also named Philip was married to Herodias and living in Rome. Herodias was the daughter of Aristobulus IV, yet another son of Herod the Great.

When Herod Antipas was visiting Rome, he fell in love with his half-brother's wife (who also happened to be his half-niece), and they began a torrid affair. Eventually Herodias demanded Antipas divorce his politically expedient wife, the daughter of King Aretas IV of the Nabateans, and marry her instead. And he did. John the Baptist confronted Antipas about this immorality, and so the Tetrarch arrested John and threw him in the dungeon of a remote desert fortress called Machaerus, which overlooked the Dead Sea. Recent excavations at Machaerus have uncovered two banquet halls in the Herodian fortress-palace, which fits well with Matthew's description of this lavish birthday feast.

Antipas was conflicted about John. On the one hand he wanted to kill him, but he was afraid of how people would react. On the other hand, Mark tells us the Tetrarch recognized John was a holy man and liked listening to John's teaching. He also tells us John's continued criticism of their marriage drove Herodias crazy, and she was looking for a way to kill him. (See Mark 6:17-20.) When Antipas' birthday party got out of hand, she was able to manipulate the Tetrarch into beheading John. When Jesus heard the news, he withdrew to be alone.

Clearly, Jesus grieved the brutal execution of his cousin, whom he had known even before they were born. (See Luke 1:39-41.) Jesus said, *"among those born of women no one is greater than John."* (Luke 7:28) We see Jesus did not ignore his grief or cover it up with pious clichés; he faced his pain head-on. We also see that Jesus did not wallow in his grief or use it as an excuse to ignore the Father's will. When the crowd found him, Jesus showed them compassion despite his grief.

Both Jesus and John gave us powerful examples to follow. John refused to hold back or sugar-coat the challenging truth God called him to declare, even when it cost him his freedom and ultimately his life. Jesus refused to let his grief over John's death poison his soul with repressed pain. He also refused to let his grief keep him from continuing to do what he saw the Father doing, no matter the cost. Both examples take faith and courage to follow. Both result in significant good fruit that lasts. Both involve different kinds of sacrifice.

What is the corrupt power God is calling you to confront with truth? How does John's example inspire you and give you courage? What pain or grief is God calling you to face? What do you need to push through so it does not hinder your mission? How does Jesus' example inspire you and give you courage?

REFLECT AND RESPOND
What is Jesus saying to me right now?

What step of faith is Jesus calling me to take today?

Footsteps Every Week: Review

Write a brief summary of what Jesus said to you each day this past week and the step of faith he called you to take:

Monday

Tuesday

Wednesday

Thursday

Friday

Saturday

Footsteps Every Week: Reflect

Big Picture
As you look over what Jesus has said to you this past week, do you see any themes? What is the most important thing you need to remember and believe?

Predictable Pattern
As you look over what Jesus called you to do this past week, is there a new predictable pattern he is inviting you to establish in your life with God and others?

Plant the Word
As you look over the readings from this past week, write out the passage that feels most important for you and memorize it over the next week:

DAY 37

READ AND LISTEN: MATTHEW 14:15-21
Take a minute to listen for what the Spirit is saying in these verses…

COMMENT AND CONSIDER
We live in a society where nothing is ever enough. No matter what grades we get, we always feel we could have done better. No matter how high the stock market goes, we are always worried that it won't go higher. No matter how much money we have in the bank, we are always afraid it will run out. Nothing is ever enough.

Jesus demonstrates a fundamentally different mindset. After a season of grief and mission, he took the disciples away to a deserted place for a time of rest and renewal. Ancient tradition says this was the lush area about a mile west of Capernaum called Tabgha, where seven springs water grass and trees at the shore of the lake, even today. But when the crowds found them there, Jesus saw they were like sheep without a shepherd, and he began to heal them. Although he was depleted, Jesus operated out of an overflow of the abundance he received from his deep connection to the Father.

The disciples saw the staggering need of the crowds and felt overwhelmed. When Jesus challenged them to feed the hungry crowd, they must have laughed out loud. Or cried. *"We only have five loaves and two fish."* They calculated the catering cost for 15,000 hungry mouths and knew they didn't have enough. Not by a long shot. What they didn't know was that the Father is always enough.

Jesus didn't condemn them for their lack of faith, but he showed them a better way. He demonstrated how to operate by faith out of an abundance mindset rather than a scarcity mindset. He didn't take the boy's lunch and give it to the people. He gave it to his heavenly Father first.

When Matthew tells us he "blessed" the food, it means he prayed the traditional prayer, "Blessed are you Lord our God, King of the Universe, who brings forth bread from the earth…" Jesus was showing them what happens when we offer our measly resources to the One who created all things by his Word and who sustains all things by his power. He was reminding them that our Dad is the King of the Universe and is always enough no matter the need!

Notice Jesus didn't give the food to the hungry crowd himself; he had his disciples do it. He wanted them to learn how to exercise the faith his word was planting in their hearts. He wanted them to understand God's impossible math—how he can multiply our insufficient resources into an overabundance in the face of overwhelming need. He was moving them from a scarcity mindset focused on what they didn't have, to an abundance mindset focused on what their Father the King always has. And as they waded into the hungry crowd and kept breaking off pieces of bread and fish, they experienced the miracle happening through them. They saw that what they had to offer was more than enough when they stepped out in faith, trusting that their Father is more than enough.

What mindset do you currently have? Are you focused on what you don't have or what your Father the King always has? Are you trying to do it yourself and coming up short, or trusting your Father who is always enough?

Reflect and Respond

What is Jesus saying to me right now?

What step of faith is Jesus calling me to take today?

DAY 38

READ AND LISTEN: MATTHEW 14:22-36
Take a minute to listen for what the Spirit is saying in these verses…

COMMENT AND CONSIDER
In yesterday's reading we saw Jesus trust that the Father's abundance was enough, even in his depleted state. But this doesn't mean Jesus abandoned his predictable patterns of rest. Since the crowd found them in their deserted place of rest and the Father called them to minister to the crowd, Jesus took the next opportunity to rest and abide with the Father.

Jesus is showing us two complementary truths. We must never turn healthy rhythms into legalistic idols. We must always be ready to do what the Father is prompting us to do by his Spirit. But we must also ferociously guard our times of rest and abiding, lest the enemy steal away this gift and leave us in a place of burnout and unfruitfulness. Jesus was always ready to do whatever he saw the Father doing, but he was also determined to maintain healthy rhythms of abiding in order to bear good fruit that lasts.

So Jesus sent the disciples on ahead and retreated up the mountain for a night of prayer and abiding with the Father. An ancient cave on the hillside above Tabgha, the place of seven springs, has been associated with his night of prayer. Finally, Jesus was alone. But as morning was about to dawn, he knew his disciples were struggling on the water and needed him. So, he did what the laws of physics tell us cannot be done. He came to them walking on the water! Jesus was so filled from his time with the Father that his faith had become stronger than gravity.

Seeing Jesus on the water was so far outside their experience that the disciples were terrified. But Jesus reassured them it was him, and Peter reacted as every true disciple should. He wanted to learn how to do everything Jesus did. He was ready to imitate his Rabbi, even in this impossible thing. This is the heart of true discipleship. And so Jesus said, *"Come."* As Peter stepped out of the boat, his gaze was fixed on Jesus, and faith was keeping him afloat! But when he began to focus on the waves and the wind all around him, his faith fizzled, and he began to sink. Jesus did not abandon him but caught him and pulled him back up. *"You of little faith, why did you doubt?"*

Jesus showed the disciples that his source of power was in his deep connection to the Father. The same can be true for us. As we abide with Jesus and keep our eyes fixed on him, we will be able to follow his example by faith, even in the impossible things. Peter didn't do it perfectly, but for a minute he was walking on water! It was not Jesus' divinity that allowed him to overcome the law of gravity; it was his faith in the Father. As we exercise faith in Jesus and keep following his footsteps, we will find ourselves overcoming normal human expectations and doing the very things Jesus did. We won't do it perfectly, but when we fail and begin to sink, Jesus will meet us amid our storms to pull us back up.

Are you willing to do whatever you see the Father doing, even if it doesn't fit your plan? Are you determined to keep predictable patterns of abiding with Jesus so you can bear good fruit that lasts? What "impossible" thing is Jesus calling you to do, following his example by faith?

Reflect and Respond
What is Jesus saying to me right now?

What step of faith is Jesus calling me to take today?

DAY 39

READ AND LISTEN: MATTHEW 15:1-20
Take a minute to listen for what the Spirit is saying in these verses…

COMMENT AND CONSIDER
The Pharisees were an elite group of rabbis who were especially zealous, not just for the written Law of the Hebrew Bible, but for the interpretations of various rabbis that had been passed down for generations. These religious traditions became even more important to the Pharisees than the revealed Law given to Moses at Mount Sinai. About 170 years after the time of Jesus, these oral interpretations were written down in the Mishnah, which became the heart of the Talmud, which is still the primary text of Orthodox Judaism today. But in the first century they were memorized and passed down verbally from rabbi to disciple, which is why they were referred to as the "Oral Law."

Jesus was deeply committed to the revealed Word of God in the Hebrew Scriptures, but he rejected the Oral Law as binding and did not follow it or teach his disciples to do so. This was a primary cause of conflict between Jesus and the Pharisees. Matthew tells us that a group of Pharisees from Jerusalem confronted Jesus asking why his disciples were not following their specific hand-washing rules. These rules were not about actually cleaning dirt off their hands. They were symbolic in nature and part of the religious classification of people as "clean" or "unclean."

Jesus responded by asking these Pharisees why they placed a greater importance on their religious traditions than the revealed Word of God in the written Law. He even gave an example of how they justified breaking the commandment to honor your father and mother with their teaching that a financial gift dedicated to the Temple was more important than providing financial support to parents in their old age. As Jesus said, *"In this way, you have nullified the word of God because of your tradition. Hypocrites!"* And then he quoted Isaiah 29:13 as a prophecy predicting their preference of human traditions over God's revealed Word.

Then Jesus turned to the crowd who was watching them and took his criticism a step further. He challenged the entire system of kosher foods when he said, *"It's not what goes into the mouth that defiles a person, but what comes out of the mouth—this defiles a person."* This radical declaration was scandalous to the Jewish religious establishment. Jesus made a distinction between the symbolic laws of the Old Testament, which were designed to mark the people of Israel as distinct from the pagan cultures that surrounded them, and the moral laws of the Old Testament, which express universal truths for all people and all times.

Even Jesus' disciples had a hard time understanding and accepting what Jesus was saying, which is why they pointed out that the Pharisees were scandalized by Jesus' statements—the Greek verb translated *"took offense"* in v. 12 is *skandalizo*. When Jesus stated that these Pharisees were blind guides who would be uprooted by God, Peter just couldn't wrap his mind around it. Jesus explained that it is from a corrupt heart that sinful and truly unclean thoughts and actions flow, not from external rituals devised by humans. Jesus points us away from an over-ritualized religion to an examination of our deepest thoughts and intentions.

In what ways have you slipped into prioritizing familiar traditions over seeking God's will, no matter how challenging it might be? Are you prepared to go deeper than your external actions and examine the thoughts and intentions of your heart?

Reflect and Respond

What is Jesus saying to me right now?

What step of faith is Jesus calling me to take today?

DAY 40

READ AND LISTEN: MATTHEW 15:21-28
Take a minute to listen for what the Spirit is saying in these verses…

COMMENT AND CONSIDER
Jesus cast a scandalously universal vision of God's Kingdom in which both Jews and Gentiles are welcomed into God's family. This is what almost got him killed in Nazareth. Although he demonstrated a shocking openness to Samaritans and Gentiles, his missional strategy was to focus on the everyday Jewish people who lived in the small towns of Galilee. After his resurrection he told his disciples they were the ones who were commissioned to go to the ends of the earth and make disciples of all nations.

Periodically Jesus took his disciples on retreats completely out of their familiar Jewish mission field to the largely Gentile areas to the north and east. Mark tells us this was so that no one would recognize and disturb them during these much-needed times of rest and renewal. (See Mark 7:24.)

In this case Jesus took his disciples on a retreat up the coast north of Israel to the regions of the great Phoenician cites of Tyre and Sidon in present-day Lebanon. Although they were seeking anonymity, a Canaanite woman recognized them and cried out to Jesus, referring to him with the Messianic title "Son of David," and asking him to deliver her daughter from demonization. When the disciples asked him to send her away, Jesus simply reiterated his missional strategy, saying, *"I was sent only to the lost sheep of the house of Israel."*

When the woman knelt before Jesus begging for his help, he set an even stronger boundary to protect the disciples' time of rest, saying, *"It isn't right to take the children's bread and throw it to the dogs."* In Middle Eastern culture, dogs are considered dirty and dangerous because they often live as feral scavengers and randomly attack people. This was a relatively harsh thing for

Jesus to say to this woman, particularly because it was a term of derision used by both Jews and Gentiles to express antipathy towards one another.

However, this Gentile woman demonstrated her faith in Jesus and her determination to get help for her daughter when she turned the image into a positive one, saying, *"Yes, Lord, yet even the dogs eat the crumbs that fall from their masters' table."* She envisioned a domesticated guard dog that lives inside the home, has an endearing relationship with her "master," and is allowed to eat the scraps falling from the table where the children eat their meals. Jesus recognized the strength and sincerity of her faith and realized this was one of those instances when the Father was doing something despite his plan for rest, so he decided to heal her daughter.

This Canaanite woman is a beautiful example of courage, humility, and stubborn faith. Like her, we are called to come to Jesus in faith, seeking what we need most. As Jesus said in his parables on prayer, persistence is the key to seeing real breakthrough when we are up against impossible obstacles. When we keep knocking, seeking, and asking, we find the door will eventually open, just as it was for this amazing woman.

What obstacle are you unable to overcome by your own strength? How are you coming to Jesus seeking his deliverance? Are you willing to be as determined and persistent as this woman was?

Reflect and Respond

What is Jesus saying to me right now?

What step of faith is Jesus calling me to take today?

DAY 41

READ AND LISTEN: MATTHEW 15:29-39

Take a minute to listen for what the Spirit is saying in these verses…

COMMENT AND CONSIDER

Matthew and Mark both record two miraculous feedings. In the first Jesus fed five thousand people with five loaves and two fish. In this second one he fed four thousand with seven loaves and "a few" fish. In the first feeding there were twelve baskets of bread left over. In this second one there were seven baskets. The first feeding seemingly took place in the primarily Jewish area of Tabgha on the northwest shore of the lake. The second seems to be on the northeast shore, near Bethsaida, on the primarily Gentile side of the lake.

The differing numbers of leftover loaves have often been understood symbolically, with the twelve loaves left on the Jewish side pointing to the twelve tribes of Israel and the seven loaves left on the Gentile side pointing to the completeness of God including the Gentiles in his Kingdom. But Luke and John only record one miraculous feeding of five thousand men using five loaves and two fish with twelve baskets of bread left over, and they seem to locate the feeding on the primarily Gentile northeast shore of the lake. It is clear the Gospel writers are recording a selective account of what Jesus did, so it is not surprising to find only one miraculous feeding in Luke and John, but the lack of geographical clarity makes it harder to interpret the number of leftover baskets as pointing to Jews versus Gentiles.

While the location and the number of leftover baskets differed, the pattern was the same:

- In compassion Jesus is concerned for the well-being of the hungry crowds.
- He asks the disciples to provide food for them.
- The disciples protest that it is impractical for them to buy that much food.

- Jesus asks how much food they do have.
- Jesus offers this insufficient amount up to God with thanks.
- Jesus instructs the disciples to distribute the bread and fish.
- The crowd is fed and there are still baskets of bread left over.

As we noted in the first miraculous feeding, Jesus had the disciples participate in the miracle. From the perspective of discipleship this makes perfect sense. Rabbis trained their disciples by verbally teaching and visually modeling their way of life, allowing the disciples to listen and observe, and then calling them to participate and imitate this way of life. Through this process the rabbi trained his disciples to know what he knew and do what he did, and so become rabbis like him.

One aspect of the Way of Jesus is learning how to allow the supernatural power of God to flow through you as it flowed through Jesus in order to do God's will on earth as it is in heaven. Jesus-shaped disciples will learn how to operate in the supernatural power of God so they can do his will, just as Jesus did. In this case, Jesus showed his disciples how to look to God for the power they needed to do his will, then step out in faith and act as if God's power would come. It must have been scary for them to wade into a hungry crowd with such insufficient resources, but they took a step of faith and the power of God flowed through them to do the impossible!

Have you ever experienced a supernatural miracle? Do you know how to let God's power flow through you? What step of faith is Jesus calling you to take so that you would be supernaturally empowered to do his will?

Reflect and Respond
What is Jesus saying to me right now?

What step of faith is Jesus calling me to take today?

DAY 42

READ AND LISTEN: MATTHEW 16:1-12
Take a minute to listen for what the Spirit is saying in these verses…

COMMENT AND CONSIDER
In this passage we see the religious leaders weren't really open to Jesus. They asked him for a sign from heaven when Jesus had been giving them countless signs! He was teaching with authority, telling profound parables, casting out demons, walking on water, calming storms, feeding multitudes, and healing every kind of illness and injury. As Matthew puts it, *"So the crowd was amazed when they saw those unable to speak talking, the crippled restored, the lame walking, and the blind seeing, and they gave glory to the God of Israel."* (Matthew 15:31)

Jesus responded to this request of the Pharisees and Sadducees by quoting a common saying about how to read the weather. Still today people say, "Red sky at night, sailor's delight. Red sky in morning, sailors take warning." If mariners can look at the sky and see what is happening with the weather, how much more should these religious leaders have been able see the Kingdom of God was breaking into their world? But Jesus knew that, no matter how many miracles he performed, it wouldn't open their hardened hearts and closed minds. Referring to Jonah's three days in the belly of the whale, he hoped his own three days in the tomb and subsequent resurrection would be enough to break through to them.

This is a reminder that some people will never be convinced no matter how many miracles they see because their hearts and minds are not open. This is why Jesus tells us to shake the dust off our feet and move on when people are not receptive to our friendship and our faith. (See Matthew 10:14.) It is also a reminder of how easy it is to relate to Jesus more as a consumer than as a disciple. A consumer simply wants Jesus to do things for them. A disciple wants to be close to Jesus and become like him; they submit and follow his example. Clearly the Pharisees and Sadducees had no interest in submitting and following, so Jesus *"left them and went away."*

After he and the disciples sailed across the lake, Jesus warned them not to be affected by the example of the Pharisees and Sadducees. This *"leaven"* Jesus spoke of is the insidious influence of the people and the culture around us that reflects the values of the kingdoms of this world rather than the coming Kingdom of God. This is what I call "bad discipleship," meaning all the examples that lead us away from the Way of Jesus and shape us into a different image than his. We need to make sure we are actually submitting to and following Jesus so we can be the light that shines in the darkness and the salt that seasons the earth, not the other way around.

And yet the disciples still didn't get it. So, Jesus patiently explained he was not talking about leaven in the literal bread they had seen multiplied, but the subtle influence of those who refuse to receive the Good News of the Kingdom. And finally, they understood. It is good to know that Jesus will keep patiently explaining the Kingdom to those with an open heart and mind!

Who do you need to walk away from because they are a bad example? Who or what has a subtle influence over you that is shaping you according to the kingdoms of this world more than the Kingdom of God? What does it mean for you to keep submitting to and following Jesus even when you don't fully understand him?

Reflect and Respond

What is Jesus saying to me right now?

What step of faith is Jesus calling me to take today?

Footsteps Every Week: Review

Write a brief summary of what Jesus said to you each day this past week and the step of faith he called you to take:

Monday

Tuesday

Wednesday

Thursday

Friday

Saturday

Footsteps Every Week: Reflect

Big Picture
As you look over what Jesus has said to you this past week, do you see any themes? What is the most important thing you need to remember and believe?

Predictable Pattern
As you look over what Jesus called you to do this past week, is there a new predictable pattern he is inviting you to establish in your life with God and others?

Plant the Word
As you look over the readings from this past week, write out the passage that feels most important for you and memorize it over the next week:

DAY 43

READ AND LISTEN: MATTHEW 16:13-28
Take a minute to listen for what God is saying in these verses…

COMMENT AND CONSIDER
Caesarea Philippi was a pagan city at the very northern tip of Israel where the Greek god Pan had been worshiped for centuries. From the mouth of a large cave flowed one of the main springs that still feeds the Jordan River today. The ancient Greeks believed this was a gateway to the underworld, guarded by Pan, the half-goat, half-human god. In front of this cave and along the adjacent cliffs stood several pagan temples and shrines where sacrifices and sexual rites were practiced.

Matthew specifies that Jesus brought his closest disciples on a retreat to *"the region of Caesarea Philippi,"* not to the pagan shrines but to the area outside the city. Not far from the cave of Pan is a lush box canyon with a beautiful waterfall at one end which fills the shady gorge with a cooling mist. We can't say for certain that this is where Jesus brought his disciples, but it is the ideal location for a time of retreat and renewal.

While resting in this beautiful area, Jesus began to ask the disciples about the rumors concerning his true identity. During this interaction Simon suddenly receives certainty that Jesus is, in fact, the long-awaited Messiah, the Son of the living God that they have been anticipating for so long! Jesus confirms his confession of faith with an incredible affirmation, *"I also say to you that you are Peter, and on this rock I will build my church, and the gates of Hades will not overpower it."* Jesus was making an obvious reference to the cave of Pan.

As a sign of their Covenant relationship, Jesus gave Simon a new name, much as we often do in marriage covenants today. The name *"Peter"* (Greek: *petros*) is the diminutive form of the word for *"rock"* (Greek; *petra*). In the Hebrew Scriptures God is often referred to as *"the rock."* (See Psalm 18.) Jesus gave Simon his own family name! He entered into Simon's family and turned them inside out, retooling their family fishing business as a Kingdom business; *"I will make you fish for people."* (Matthew 4:19)

Now Jesus invited Simon into his family, the great family of his heavenly Father, the King of the Universe. Jesus' earthly relatives were builders, stone masons, and Jesus uses this image to define his Father's family business. In his heavenly Father's family, they were building a new creation, and Jesus was inviting Simon to become a building block, shaped into his image, so he could become part of this new family, this new church.

When Jesus went on to tell them he would build this new church by going to Jerusalem and laying down his life, Peter couldn't accept it. But Jesus rebukes Peter, saying, *"Get behind me, Satan! You are a hindrance to me because you're not thinking about God's concerns but human concerns."* The word translated *"hindrance"* here (Greek: *skandalon*) describes the stone you trip over. Jesus is telling Simon that if he resists the way of the cross, he will not become a building block in God's Kingdom, but rather a stumbling stone. Then Jesus said that anyone who wants to be his disciple will have to take up a cross and follow him all the way to Golgotha.

Are you resisting the way of the cross in your life? Are you going to be a building block or a stumbling stone? What does it mean for you to take up your cross today?

Reflect and Respond
What is the Spirit saying to me right now?

What step of faith is the Spirit calling me to take today?

DAY 44

READ AND LISTEN: MATTHEW 17:1-13
Take a minute to listen for what the Spirit is saying in these verses…

COMMENT AND CONSIDER
The group of people who regularly filled up the house of Simon and Andrew in Capernaum are referred to as Jesus' "disciples." However, Jesus chose 12 of them who left their jobs and travelled with him full-time. There was an even closer inner circle of three disciples, Peter, James and John (and sometimes Andrew). Jesus invested extra time with these, his most trusted disciples, and this passage records one of those times.

We don't know to which mountain Jesus took them, but Caesarea Philippi sits at the base of Mount Hermon, the highest peak in the region, so that is a good candidate. The traditional site has been identified as Mount Tabor in the Jezreel Valley, not far from Nazareth, but there is no historical evidence for that site. In any case, while they were on this *"high mountain"* they had an experience that was difficult to describe. Jesus was *"transfigured"* (Greek: *metemorphothe*) before their very eyes.

Light radiated from Jesus' face which *"shone like the sun."* This was reminiscent of Moses' face after his encounter with God on Mount Sinai, except it was Jesus' own divinity which was the inner source of this radiant glory. (See Exodus 34:29.) Jesus' clothing became *"as white as the light."* This was reminiscent of the fiery chariot and whirlwind that carried Elijah into heaven. (See 2 Kings 2:11-12.) So perhaps it is not too surprising that both Moses and Elijah appeared alongside Jesus! God emptied himself when he took on human flesh in Jesus, and Jesus operated in his full humanity during his life on earth. But now Jesus' full divinity leaked out, and the disciples were overwhelmed with the revelation.

Peter, always the first to act, offered to build three tents, perhaps wanting to capture this incredible moment and memorialize it so it didn't slip away. But then the revelation went up another notch when they were enveloped in a cloud of glory and God the Father spoke over Jesus, *"This is my beloved Son, with whom I am well-pleased. Listen to him!"* When God appeared to the people of Israel in the time of Moses, it was often in a cloud of glory. (See Exodus 13:21-22; 40:34-38.) Finally, this was all too much to bear, and the three disciples collapsed under the weight of this radiant glory and their own fear.

Although the disciples knew Jesus in his full humanity, this was the moment when Jesus' full divinity was also revealed to them. It is difficult to hold these two aspects of Jesus' nature together. We can reduce Jesus to a really smart but merely human teacher. Or we can assume he floated around Galilee in a bubble of divine glory. In fact, during his time on earth, Jesus operated in his full humanity in order to show us how we are meant to live, but never forfeited his full divinity to which he returned after his resurrection and ascension.

The title Jesus most often applied to himself was *"the Son of Man."* This is a reference to Daniel's vision of *"one like a son of man"* who came from the throne of the Ancient of Days and descended to earth on clouds of glory. (See Daniel 7:13-14) As those who follow Jesus, we must always keep in healthy tension the fully human example Jesus has set for us while never compromising the full divinity of Jesus who is the Word become flesh, God with us, Emmanuel.

Do you tend to emphasize Jesus' full humanity or his full divinity? How can you hold these two realities together in healthy tension? How does that affect your walk with Jesus?

Reflect and Respond
What is Jesus saying to me right now?

What step of faith is Jesus calling me to take today?

DAY 45

READ AND LISTEN: MATTHEW 17:14-27
Take a minute to listen for what the Spirit is saying in these verses…

COMMENT AND CONSIDER
As Jesus and his closest three disciples came down from their mountaintop high of the transfiguration, they encountered a distraught father whose young son suffered from life-threatening seizures (literally "moonstruck"). While Jesus was up on the mountain, the disciples he left behind unsuccessfully tried to cast out the demon they discerned was the root of this boy's epilepsy. We should note Jesus and his disciples healed both physical ailments and spiritual oppression and recognized that sometimes the two were intertwined. Jesus did not blame all physical infirmities on demons as some do, but he recognized when there was a spiritual element exacerbating a physical ailment. (See Matthew 9:2.)

The disciples couldn't understand why they were unable to help this boy since they had successfully cast out demons in Jesus' name on earlier mission trips. (See Luke 10:17.) Jesus tells them it is a faith problem. He is quoted using two different words in this passage to describe a lack of faith. Jesus called the wider crowds *"unbelieving"* (literally: "no faith"), whereas he called the disciples *"you of little faith"* (literally: "inadequate faith"). These are two different issues.

"Unbelieving" means faith is absent. Paul tells us faith comes from hearing the personal word of Christ (see Romans 10:17), and the writer of Hebrews tells us without faith it is impossible to please God (see Hebrews 11:6). We can't summon faith by our own strength, but we can open our ears and our hearts to receive the word of Christ by which the Holy Spirit plants faith in us. Some people stubbornly resist faith and as a result are unable to know God personally or walk in his Spirit. This is the problem of unbelief.

"Little faith" means faith is present, but it is insufficient. This does not mean that we need more faith. Jesus makes that clear by saying all we need

is a tiny mustard seed of faith to move a mountain. (See Luke 17:5-6.) It means we need to learn how to *exercise* the faith the Holy Spirit has already planted in our hearts through the word of Christ. It is also important to note that Jesus is addressing them as a group when he points out their insufficient faith. In the phrase *"you of little faith"* the Greek word for *"you"* is plural, meaning as a community their faith had not yet grown strong enough to win this spiritual battle.

Jesus was training the disciples to do the things he did. By delivering this boy, Jesus showed them and us that we can learn to exercise faith with the authority given to us in Jesus so we can overcome the obstacles we face and carry out God's will by his supernatural power. As with anything else, this takes practice. The disciples had exercised faith earlier and experienced the power of God flowing through them to do his will. Now they came up against a situation they couldn't overcome. The solution is to keep exercising faith until it has grown strong enough to win the battle.

Faith is like a muscle. The more we exercise it, the stronger it grows. When we let it lie dormant, it begins to atrophy. Are you opening your heart to the personal word of Jesus so that faith is being planted in your heart? Are you willing to exercise your faith in Jesus so the supernatural power of God flows through you to do his will? In what area is Jesus calling you to exercise your faith today?

REFLECT AND RESPOND

What is Jesus saying to me right now?

What step of faith is Jesus calling me to take today?

DAY 46

READ AND LISTEN: MATTHEW 18:1-14

Take a minute to listen for what the Spirit is saying in these verses…

COMMENT AND CONSIDER

What makes a person great? Usually, we think of Herculean accomplishments like winning an Olympic medal or building a great organization or attaining global influence or creating a transcendent piece of art. People who attain such accomplishments become heroes and role models to the masses who emulate them because they, too, want to become great. However, Jesus told us that things work very differently in the Kingdom of Heaven.

In the ancient world, children were typically valued for the contribution they could make to the extended family business. This meant that young children were generally seen as a liability rather than an asset. They were also incredibly vulnerable since infant and child mortality rates were so high. In the first century, more than a quarter of infants died in their first year of life, and nearly half of all children died before reaching puberty. As a result, parents did not typically become emotionally attached to young children, recognizing there was a good chance they wouldn't survive.

With this in mind, it was shocking for Jesus to lift up a small child as the exemplar of greatness in God's Kingdom. It was the last thing anyone would have expected. Jesus specified childlike humility as a key marker of greatness, and he called his disciples to intentionally imitate children in this way. Being a disciple of Jesus means releasing control and submitting yourself to him in all things as a child trusts her parents.

In Jesus' world children were thought of as having little value. And those who submit and follow the Way of Jesus will rarely be thought of as impressive or important by the world's standards of greatness. Jesus himself came to the end of his life rejected, tortured, and nailed to a cross. And yet Jesus is, without doubt, the greatest person who ever lived! So it will be for those who follow in his footsteps.

Jesus not only lifted up a little child as a role model for the rest of us, but he applied the image to child-like disciples whom he called *"these little ones."* Jesus pointed out that those who make disciples are like spiritual parents who have a parental responsibility to protect and provide for their spiritual children. When you visit excavated first-century towns and villages in Galilee today, you nearly always see huge, circular stones turned by donkeys and used to crush olives or grind flour. If one of these were tied around your neck and thrown into the lake, you would go into the lake too and would never breathe air again! Jesus said this would be a better fate than what awaits those who fail to care for their spiritual children.

Then Jesus shifted the image to a shepherd's responsibility for his sheep. Even one lost sheep is worth whatever cost and risks it takes to return them safely to the fold, and a cause for great rejoicing when they do. We see here a powerful image of our call to care for and love those entrusted to our leadership. To be a disciple of Jesus is to become like a little child. To make Jesus-shaped disciples is to function as a responsible spiritual parent, caring for and protecting our disciples as if they were our own children. Discipleship is spiritual shepherding.

Are you willing to become more childlike in your life of discipleship? Are you willing to take spiritual responsibility for others who are entrusted to your care? What does it mean for you to become both a sheep who submits and a shepherd who takes responsibility for others?

Reflect and Respond

What is Jesus saying to me right now?

What step of faith is Jesus calling me to take today?

DAY 47

READ AND LISTEN: MATTHEW 18:15-35
Take a minute to listen for what the Spirit is saying in these verses…

COMMENT AND CONSIDER
When someone wrongs us, the first instinct of our flesh is to complain about them to somebody else. It soothes our hurt feelings to receive sympathy and invite others to share in our outrage. However, it also deepens the divide between us and the person who wronged us by feeding our self-righteousness and failing to address the destructive behavior of the other. Jesus showed us a different way for spiritual family to function in God's Kingdom:

- First, we are to go directly and address the situation with the person, one on one. If they are receptive, then reconciliation can be achieved.
- If that doesn't work, then we are to take one or two others with us and address it again.
- If that doesn't work, then it is an issue that needs to come before the leaders of our community.
- If that doesn't lead to reconciliation, then that person can no longer be considered part of the spiritual family unless they repent.

The goal here is reconciliation and the restoration of healthy functioning. Failure to deal with sin and dysfunction in the church only leads to more division and poisoned fruit.

This teaching raised a question in Peter's mind, *"Lord, how many times must I forgive my brother or sister who sins against me? As many as seven times?"* Various rabbis taught that you only needed to forgive someone twice for the same offense, or at the most, four times. Sensing Jesus would have a high standard for the offering of forgiveness, Peter shot high with his guess of seven times. Jesus transcended all of this by answering *"seventy times seven."* This ridiculously high number makes the point that there is no limit to giving grace in God's Kingdom because of the limitless grace we have received from our heavenly Father. When we withhold forgiveness for whatever reason, we end up carrying a burden of resentment that poisons our soul.

To underscore this, Jesus told a parable of a man who owed a king such a ridiculously high debt that he could never have paid it off. When the king decided to freely forgive the huge debt, it should have created in this man a cheerful willingness to forgive the paltry debt owed to him by another man. Instead, he turned around and threw this man and his entire family into debtor's prison without mercy. Jesus said there is a terrible fate awaiting those who have received such grace but refuse to pass it on to others. Jesus showed us the source of true forgiveness toward one another is an awareness of just how much our heavenly Father has forgiven us. This is why Jesus taught us to pray, *"forgive us our debts, as we also have forgiven our debtors."* (Matthew 6:12)

It is important to note the difference between forgiveness and reconciliation. Forgiveness is something we extend unconditionally to others, just as it has been to us. We are called to forgive whether the other party takes ownership for their actions or not. However, reconciliation, the restoration of relationship, is only possible when both parties take responsibility for their part in what has happened, and there is genuine forgiveness and repentance.

Is there anyone who has wronged you with whom you need to seek reconciliation? Is there anyone you have wronged from whom you need to ask forgiveness? Is there anyone you need to forgive, regardless of their attitude about hurting you? How can you promote the health and fruitfulness of your spiritual family?

Reflect and Respond
What is Jesus saying to me right now?

What step of faith is Jesus calling me to take today?

DAY 48

READ AND LISTEN: MATTHEW 19:1-12
Take a minute to listen for what the Spirit is saying in these verses…

COMMENT AND CONSIDER
When we read the accounts of creation in Genesis 1 and 2, it is clear that God's good design was for human beings to be either male or female and for them to enter into a life-long, exclusive relationship of oneness and fruitfulness through sexual intercourse. Although faithful marriage is clearly God's design, the Old Testament Law allowed the husband to divorce his wife if he found something *"indecent"* about her. (See Deuteronomy 24:1.) This was to prevent women from being thrown out by their husbands with no proof that the marriage was legally terminated, which would prevent them from remarrying and leave them without protection and provision.

Rabbis had a long-running debate about what qualified as *"indecent"* and allowed a man to divorce his wife. The more conservative school of Rabbi Shammai interpreted this as sexual sin, whereas the more liberal school of Hillel said it could be something as simple as burning the dinner. Later, Rabbi Akiba of the Hillel school said a husband could divorce his wife if he saw another woman who was "fairer than she."

Jesus points back to God's intention in creation and makes it clear marriage is designed to be a permanent bond never meant to be broken. As he said, *"Therefore, what God has joined together, let no one separate."* He explained Moses' allowance for divorce was a concession to the hard-heartedness of broken people, but that it was never meant to be that way. Furthermore, he said that even if someone does divorce and then remarries another, it is as if the divorce never happened, and they are committing adultery.

In our society, where half of all marriages end in divorce, this is a very challenging teaching, as it was in the first century as well. This is why the disciples concluded maybe it is better not to marry at all. Jesus responded by admitting this view of marriage would not be accepted by everyone. He also pointed out some people will not marry, either because they suffer from malformed sexual organs, or their sexual organs have been removed, or because they choose celibacy. Although marriage between a man and woman is God's design, Jesus pointed out that marriage is not necessary to live a full and fruitful life. In fact, two of the greatest figures of the New Testament, John the Baptist and Jesus himself, never married.

Our society has two deeply divisive perspectives on marriage and sexuality. One view is that each person is free to express their sexuality and their sexual identity however they want, and it is wrong to do anything but affirm and celebrate their chosen expression. The other view is that whoever does not fit into God's ideal of a life-long, faithful marriage between a man and a woman is sinful and should be condemned. But the way of Jesus transcends both perspectives.

While Jesus holds up the highest moral standards when it comes to marriage and sexuality, he also demonstrates a shockingly gracious acceptance of people from every kind of background and lifestyle. If we can't welcome people of any sexual orientation or identity or history into our lives, then we are not following Jesus. If we compromise Jesus' moral standards to make people more comfortable, we also are not following Jesus.

How does Jesus' perspective shape your view of marriage? How does Jesus' example of welcoming sinners shape your attitude and actions toward those who don't live up to the ideal?

Reflect and Respond

What is Jesus saying to me right now?

What step of faith is Jesus calling me to take today?

Footsteps Every Week: Review

Write a brief summary of what Jesus said to you each day this past week and the step of faith he called you to take:

Monday

Tuesday

Wednesday

Thursday

Friday

Saturday

Footsteps Every Week: Reflect

Big Picture
As you look over what Jesus has said to you this past week, do you see any themes? What is the most important thing you need to remember and believe?

Predictable Pattern
As you look over what Jesus called you to do this past week, is there a new predictable pattern he is inviting you to establish in your life with God and others?

Plant the Word
As you look over the readings from this past week, write out the passage that feels most important for you and memorize it over the next week:

DAY 49

READ AND LISTEN: MATTHEW 19:13-22
Take a minute to listen for what the Spirit is saying in these verses…

COMMENT AND CONSIDER

Jesus constantly challenged people's assumptions about what is important in life. As we have seen, Jesus' approach to children was countercultural. Although the disciples tried to chase away the kids who always flocked around Jesus, he recognized their value regardless of what they could contribute to the family business, and he treated them as people of dignity, worthy of his full attention.

Similarly, his approach to material possessions was countercultural. In a society where wealth was seen as a sign of God's favor and blessing, Jesus left behind a relatively lucrative career in his family's building business and became an itinerant teacher who had no place to lay his head. He treated rich and poor alike, which is why his followers included people from every socio-economic background. When a rich young ruler came to Jesus asking what else he needed to do to have eternal life, Jesus challenged all his assumptions about what makes up a good life. The Greek word translated "young" in v. 22 means he was between 20 and 40 years old. Luke 18:18 tells us he was a "ruler," which could mean a leader in the synagogue or a city official.

Jesus confronted this rich young ruler's thinking about goodness, *"Why do you ask me about what is good?" he said to him. "There is only one who is good."* Jesus showed him that real goodness comes from our connection to God who alone is truly good. We cannot create goodness by our own moral efforts. Jesus demonstrated this point by calling the man to live up to the vision of God's Law. As Jesus pointed out in the Sermon on the Mount, God's Law demands not just outward conformity, but the transformation of our deepest thoughts and intentions to bring them into alignment with God's will. As Jesus said, *"Be perfect, therefore, as your heavenly Father is perfect."* (Matthew 5:48)

Although this man believed he was fulfilling the Law, deep down inside he knew something was still missing in his seemingly perfect life. When he asked, *"What do I still lack?"* Jesus responded with the last thing he ever expected to hear, *"Go, sell your belongings and give to the poor, and you will have treasure in heaven. Then come, follow me."* Jesus prophetically struck a nerve by identifying the very thing that was keeping this man from stepping into the Kingdom of God and following him.

Jesus was trying to show him that his many possessions had come to possess him. He wanted this man to see a life of discipleship in the Kingdom of Heaven was worth so much more than everything he owned combined. But this sharp, successful young man failed to see the treasure that was buried in that field. He wasn't willing to give up everything else to buy the one priceless pearl. He chose the worthless rags of his riches over the incalculable treasure Jesus was offering. The passage closes with a heart-wrenching description of this man's bondage to material things: *He went away grieving, because he had many possessions.*

What is keeping you from following Jesus more closely and giving him more control in your life? Are you trying to make yourself good enough for God, or are you allowing his Spirit to transform you day by day into the image of Jesus?

Reflect and Respond

What is Jesus saying to me right now?

What step of faith is Jesus calling me to take today?

DAY 50

READ AND LISTEN: MATTHEW 19:23-30
Take a minute to listen for what God is saying in these verses…

COMMENT AND CONSIDER
Watching the rich young ruler walk away sad must have impacted Jesus' disciples as they considered all they had given up to follow their Rabbi. Jesus seized this teaching moment and pointed out what a seductive idol material wealth can be in our lives. To illustrate just how strong the pull is between the riches of this world and values of God's Kingdom, he said, *it is easier for a camel to go through the eye of a needle than for a rich person to enter the kingdom of God.* Considering the camel was the largest land animal in Palestine at the time of Jesus, and the eye of needle was the smallest opening in the typical home, it is a hilariously vivid picture of impossibility!

Some have pointed out that there was a gate in Jerusalem called "the eye of the needle" that was so low that camels had to get down on their knees to enter the city. However, references to this gate date from the Crusader period, more than a thousand years after Jesus, and mostly likely indicate the gate was named after Jesus' saying, not the other way around. It is clear from the disciples' response that they understand Jesus is giving a picture of something that is literally impossible. If it is that hard for rich people to enter the Kingdom, then how will anyone be saved and enter the Kingdom?

Jesus said, *"With man this is impossible, but with God all things are possible."* He wanted them to understand that any human effort apart from the grace and power of God will fall short in making us right with him. But the Good News for rich people is that God can fit camels through the eye of a needle! As the angel Gabriel said to Mary when announcing her miraculous conception, *"For nothing will be impossible with God."* (Luke 1:37)

It is easy to read this passage and associate the label "rich" with someone else. But those of us who live in North America need to remember that we live in one of the wealthiest societies in the history of the world. Unless you are near the bottom of the socio-economic ladder in this context, you and I would certainly be considered "rich" according to first-century standards. This means we need to take this warning from Jesus to heart. Our relative material wealth is a danger to our spiritual condition. It doesn't mean possessions are bad, but it does mean we need to be vigilant to make sure we don't allow our financial security and material comforts to keep us from seeking God's Kingdom first and following Jesus no matter what the cost.

Halfway through this passage, the focus shifts from the rich young ruler to the disciples who have decided to give up their financial security and material comforts in order to follow Jesus. Peter asks the question everyone else is thinking: *"What will there be for us?"* Jesus didn't condemn him for asking this very honest question. Instead, he gave the incredible promise that the treasure hidden in the field is worth incalculably more than everything they had given up times one hundred! In fact, Jesus says, we will be restored to our rightful place as those who rule over God's creation and represent him in all things, which is a life richer and more abundant than we can even begin to imagine!

How are your financial security and material comforts competing with Jesus' call in your life? Can believing Jesus' promise make you more bold as his Kingdom-seeking disciple?

Reflect and Respond
What is Jesus saying to me right now?

What step of faith is Jesus calling me to take today?

DAY 51

READ AND LISTEN: MATTHEW 20:1-16

Take a minute to listen for what the Spirit is saying in these verses...

COMMENT AND CONSIDER

In the ancient world, as in parts of the developing world today, the workday is defined by the sun. When the sun comes up about 6 AM, the day begins. When the sun goes down around 6 PM, your work is done. Jesus tells a parable about day laborers and their wages that shows us something about the Kingdom of Heaven. If you drive into the parking lot of The Home Depot near my house, you will see men standing around waiting to be hired for the day. This was an ancient practice as well. It is harvest time, and the owner of a vineyard needs workers to bring in his harvest before the grapes go bad, so he goes to the marketplace, his equivalent of The Home Depot, around 6 AM and hires some men to work for the day.

The normal daily wage for a laborer was one silver coin called a denarius, which is what the owner agrees to pay these workers. As the day wears on, the vineyard owner sees more workers hanging around the marketplace *"doing nothing,"* and so he decides to hire more people around nine in the morning, noon, and three o'clock in the afternoon. He promises he will pay them *"whatever is right,"* presumably meaning they will get the proportion of a denarius that reflects the portion of the day they will work. Finally, in the eleventh hour, the owner sees yet more workers *"standing around"* and so he hires them as well, even though there is only one hour of sunlight left.

Jesus' language implies that the vineyard owner is not hiring extra workers because he needs them. He would have known how many men he needed from the beginning. It sounds as if he is hiring them because they don't have work, and so he gives them an opportunity to work. This is a hint at the owner's generous character. The punchline of the parable comes at sundown when the owner instructs his vineyard manager to pay the workers, starting with those who were hired last.

The manager pays those who worked one hour a full denarius, which was shockingly generous because it represents twelve times what the fair wage would have been! The workers who started work at 6 AM and endured the heat of the day anticipate a similar windfall but are disappointed to be paid the same single denarius. When they complain, the owner reminds them he is paying them exactly what he promised. As he says, *Are you jealous because I'm generous?* This phrase reads literally, "Is your eye evil?" When we can't see the nature of God's Kingdom, we can't rejoice in God's generosity.

Once again Jesus shows us that the Kingdom of God operates differently than the kingdoms of this world. In our world you have to earn what you are paid. At least in theory, your wage represents the amount of work you have expended. In the Kingdom of Heaven, you receive according to the generosity of the owner of the vineyard, not according to the amount of effort you have put in. From a worldly perspective this seems unfair, but the story shows us that God is more than fair. He is gracious and merciful and gives us far more than we deserve.

How do you compare yourself to others? Do you ever feel that God "owes" you something? How does this parable challenge your perspective?

Reflect and Respond

What is Jesus saying to me right now?

What step of faith is Jesus calling me to take today?

DAY 52

READ AND LISTEN: MATTHEW 20:17-28
Take a minute to listen for what the Spirit is saying in these verses…

COMMENT AND CONSIDER
This was the third time Jesus told his disciples he would suffer, die, and rise again. This took on a heightened sense of danger because Jesus specified it would happen in Jerusalem, the very place they were heading. In this ominous context, Matthew reports that the mother of James and John asked Jesus to give her sons special status. She obviously did not understand what Jesus was saying!

The Gospels list the women disciples who were at the cross when Jesus was being crucified. Mark names Mary Magdalene, another Mary who is the mother of James and Joses, and Salome. (See Mark 15:40-41.) Matthew lists these women at the cross, naming the two Marys as well as an unnamed mother of James and John, the sons of Zebedee. (See Matthew 27:56.) This unnamed woman seems to be Salome, the mother of James and John. John lists the two previous Marys, Mary the mother of Jesus, and *"Mary's sister."* (John 19:25) It seems likely this unnamed sister of Mary is Salome, the mother of James and John and wife of Zebedee. If so, this means James and John are Jesus' cousins.

This would mean the mother of James and John is Salome, Jesus' aunt, which explains why she would approach Jesus and ask that her sons be given a special place at his right and left hand in his Kingdom. In first-century culture, where extended family was your primary identity, it was common for relatives to be given preferential treatment. It was also common for a mother to petition on behalf of her sons. But in this case, Salome demonstrates how far she is from understanding Jesus and his Kingdom. Jesus was not heading to Herod's great palace in Jerusalem, but rather to a brutal cross erected on a rock called Golgotha just outside the city walls.

Jesus told Salome and her sons he could not promise them positions of special status, but that they would share in his experience of suffering if they chose to follow him. *"Are you able to drink the cup that I am about to drink?"* The other disciples were upset with James and John for trying to leverage their family connections to gain special status, but Jesus used this as another teaching moment for all the disciples. He explained to them that the way leadership works in the Kingdom of God is fundamentally different from the way it works in the Roman Empire and the other kingdoms of the surrounding culture.

In the kingdoms of this world, leaders use their power to control others and hold onto that power by keeping people dependent upon them. Jesus showed them a fundamentally different way by lifting each of them up, training and empowering them to do everything that he did. Jesus-shaped leadership is marked by giving power away, serving those you lead, and laying down your life to set people free. This is how Jesus led his disciples, and this is how they in turn were to lead their disciples.

In the end Salome stood at the foot of Golgotha and watched Jesus die on the cross. Eventually James was beheaded by Herod Agrippa, and John was exiled to the island of Patmos. But they learned to lead by laying down their lives. Are you looking for a place of comfort, status, and power in God's Kingdom, or are you ready to lay down your life to raise up, empower, and release others into all they are called to do?

Reflect and Respond
What is Jesus saying to me right now?

What step of faith is Jesus calling me to take today?

DAY 53

READ AND LISTEN: MATTHEW 20:29-21:11
Take a minute to listen for what the Spirit is saying in these verses...

COMMENT AND CONSIDER
The prophet Nathan prophesied that God would raise up one of King David's descendants as God's own son to rule an eternal kingdom. (See 2 Samuel 7:12–16.) This and other prophecies were the basis for the Jewish expectation of a coming *Messiah* (Hebrew for "Anointed One") who would destroy Israel's enemies once and for all and establish an eternal reign of peace. Through the successive pagan invasions and occupations of Israel, the Jewish expectation and longing for the coming of the Messiah grew more intense.

When the blind men beside the road outside of Jericho began crying out *"Lord, have mercy on us, Son of David!"* they were expressing this pent-up longing for the coming of the Messiah. Isaiah prophesied that the Messiah would give sight to the blind, as Jesus himself read in the synagogue of Nazareth. (See Isaiah 29:18; 35:5; 42:7; Luke 4:18.) When John the Baptist sent his disciples to ask Jesus if he was the Messiah, Jesus responded, *"Go and report to John what you hear and see: The blind receive their sight..."* (Matthew 11:4-5) If Jesus was in fact David's son, the anointed Son of God, these blind men expected he would restore their sight. And that is exactly what Jesus did!

Jesus and his disciples departed Jericho and made the final leg of their journey up to Jerusalem, a full day's journey, rising some 3000 feet in elevation. As they approached the Holy City, Jesus chose to make a deliberately dramatic entrance into Jerusalem. The prophet Zechariah had foretold that the Messiah would appear on the Mount of Olives and enter Jerusalem *"riding on a donkey, on a colt, the foal of a donkey."* (Zechariah 9:9, 14:4) Jesus made arrangements for a young donkey and its mother to be ready for his entrance into the city. By choosing to enter Jerusalem on the back of a young donkey, Jesus clearly demonstrated for all to see that he is the long-awaited Messiah King foretold by the prophets who had come to establish God's eternal Kingdom!

The crowds of pilgrims making their way to Jerusalem for the Passover festival understood exactly what Jesus was doing. Laying down their cloaks and the palm branches they were carrying was like rolling out the red carpet for their King. Echoing the cries of the blind men in Jericho, they shouted *"Hosanna to the Son of David! Blessed is he who comes in the name of the Lord! Hosanna in the highest heaven!"* When pilgrims made the final ascent to Jerusalem, they would begin singing the Hallel Psalms (Psalms 113-118). *"Hosanna"* is a Hebrew expression that means "O save us!" This cry of the crowd is taken from Psalm 118:25-26 and is an explicitly Messianic plea, blessing the coming King and begging him to save them!

The crowds rightly recognized Jesus as their King, but they didn't understand what kind of King he was or the nature of his Kingdom. They assumed he would throw Pontius Pilate out of Herod's Palace, wage a war against Rome, and drive out all their legions. Little did they know their King was coming to lay down his life. Little did they know it was the power of self-giving love that would conquer, not only Rome, but ultimately the whole world!

Are you ready to receive Jesus as your true King today? Do you recognize him for the kind of King he really is? Are you ready to lay down your life as he did so that his Kingdom can come through your life today?

REFLECT AND RESPOND

What is God saying to me right now?

What step of faith is God calling me to take today?

DAY 54

READ AND LISTEN: MATTHEW 21:12-22
Take a minute to listen for what the Spirit is saying in these verses…

COMMENT AND CONSIDER
After Jesus made his dramatic entrance into Jerusalem, the people were in an uproar saying, *"This is the prophet Jesus from Nazareth in Galilee."* (Matthew 21:11) Sometimes God instructed the prophets of Israel to carry out strange acts to demonstrate a prophetic warning or judgment against his people. He told Jeremiah to smash a clay pot as a demonstration of the destruction that would soon come. (See Jeremiah 19:1-13.) He told Ezekiel to make a model of Jerusalem and then lay siege to it before the people. (See Ezekiel 4:1-3.) God even told Hosea to marry a prostitute to demonstrate his unconditional love for his people! (See Hosea 1:2-3.) When Jesus strode into the huge courts of the Temple Mount, he was operating in this same prophetic mode.

Herod the Great had rebuilt the Temple and greatly expanded the surrounding courts in an effort to curry favor with the people. Across the southern end of the Temple platform, he built an enormous building called the Royal Stoa, which was where sacrificial animals were sold and various currencies exchanged for the Tyrian shekels required to pay the Temple tax. Nothing was intrinsically wrong with these sales—in fact, they were necessary for people to participate in the sacrificial system. But Jesus prophetically demonstrated God's judgement against the corruption of the Temple leadership and the exclusivism of the various barriers that prevented Gentiles, the blind, the lame, and those considered unclean from drawing near to God. This was an incredibly provocative act because it was a direct challenge to the wealthy and powerful priestly families who controlled the Temple functions.

It is no coincidence that Jesus followed his prophetic act in the Temple by gathering the blind and lame to himself in those same courts and healing them, a powerful demonstration that in his Kingdom everyone has direct access to God's transforming presence! The children who witnessed these miracles echoed the messianic shout from the Mount of Olives, *"Hosanna to the Son of David!"* The religious leaders, on the other hand, reacted with indignation to the proclamation of the children. Jesus simply responded by quoting Psalm 8:2: *"Yes, have you never read: You have prepared praise from the mouths of infants and nursing babies?"*

The next morning, after spending the night with the family of Mary, Martha, and Lazarus in Bethany on the far side of the Mount of Olives, Jesus returned to the Temple Mount. Passing a fruitless fig tree, he cursed it and the tree withered. This was not just Jesus being grumpy! It was another prophetic act in which Jesus demonstrated God's judgment of the fruitless, exclusive, and ritualistic religion being carried out on the Temple Mount. In fact, some 40 years later the Romans laid siege to Jerusalem and destroyed the Temple, tearing down every single magnificent structure which Herod had built on the mountaintop of Zion. The Temple has never been rebuilt to this day.

It is easy for the religious structures we build to support our spiritual life to become more important than our relationship with God. It is easy for these structures to become barriers rather than supports to people outside our community. How would Jesus respond to the religious culture of your church today? Are there things that need to be overturned to give people more direct access to the transforming presence of God? In what way is Jesus calling you to turn over some tables?

Reflect and Respond
What is Jesus saying to me right now?

What step of faith is Jesus calling me to take today?

Footsteps Every Week: Review

Write a brief summary of what Jesus said to you each day this past week and the step of faith he called you to take:

Monday

Tuesday

Wednesday

Thursday

Friday

Saturday

Footsteps Every Week: Reflect

Big Picture
As you look over what Jesus has said to you this past week, do you see any themes? What is the most important thing you need to remember and believe?

Predictable Pattern
As you look over what Jesus called you to do this past week, is there a new predictable pattern he is inviting you to establish in your life with God and others?

Plant the Word
As you look over the readings from this past week, write out the passage that feels most important for you and memorize it over the next week:

DAY 55

READ AND LISTEN: MATTHEW 21:23-32
Take a minute to listen for what the Spirit is saying in these verses…

COMMENT AND CONSIDER
Authority is being given the power to make decisions and enforce those decisions with definitive action. Jesus' prophetic act and healings in the Temple courts were a direct challenge to the authority of the chief priests who oversaw and ran the sacrificial system. So it is no surprise that they confronted Jesus about the basis of his authority the next day. *"By what authority are you doing these things? Who gave you this authority?"*

Jesus knew he had to walk a thin line between openly revealing his true identity and preventing the religious authorities from arresting him before he completed the tasks the Father had given him to do. For that reason, Jesus answered with a question, as he often did. He asked them from where John the Baptist's authority came—human beings or God? The chief priests and members of the Sanhedrin knew Jesus had painted them into a political corner.

Because of John's popularity with the people, these leaders knew they couldn't deny he was authorized by God. But if they openly admitted that someone outside the official religious hierarchy could be authorized by God to act independently, it would follow that Jesus could operate in the same way. Their refusal to answer allowed Jesus to put off their question and avoid being arrested before his time. It was self-evident that Jesus operated in the authority of God because he demonstrated the power necessary to do God's will. This is why he spoke directly as a representative of God his Father rather than quoting other rabbis. This is how he could heal the broken and deliver the oppressed. Nicodemus, the Pharisee, recognized this when he said to Jesus, *"Rabbi, we know that you are a teacher who has come from God, for no one could perform these signs you do unless God were with him."* (John 3:2)

Then Jesus told a parable about the nature of true authority. Of these two sons, one didn't do what he said he would do. The other one did what he said he wouldn't do. In the end it was the one who changed his mind and actually did his father's will that proved to have integrity. It is not what we say that matters most, but what we do. It is not starting with the right idea that matters most, but finishing with the truth and acting on it. It is the willingness of those who are wrong to repent and do what is right that carries authority. These are the ones authorized to represent God and act on his behalf.

The reason Jesus didn't recognize the authority of the Temple leaders is because they gave lip service to God's will but didn't have the integrity to actually do it. Even when they were confronted with proof of John's divine authority, they didn't change their minds and embrace his mission of preparation. By contrast, many tax collectors and prostitutes, who were clearly not doing God's will, responded to John by repenting and taking steps of faith to do God's will. Jesus said this is what matters most in the Kingdom of God—not where you start, but where you finish. Those who repent and believe have the authority to represent God and the power to do his will.

Are you focusing on words more than actions? Are you stuck where you began or are you willing to change your mind and do God's will as he reveals it to you? Are you humble enough to repent and believe? If so, you will carry more of the authority and power you need to do God's will.

Reflect and Respond

What is Jesus saying to me right now?

What step of faith is Jesus calling me to take today?

DAY 56

READ AND LISTEN: MATTHEW 21:33-46

Take a minute to listen for what the Spirit is saying in these verses…

COMMENT AND CONSIDER

Grapes were one of the primary crops of ancient Israel, and vineyards were a common sight. They were often protected from animals by a stone wall and from thieves by a stone watchtower. Archaeologists have discovered many such vineyards from the first century, usually with a stone platform for pressing the grapes and a vat dug in the ground to collect the juice. Jesus evoked this common image when he told a prophetic parable that foretold his own fate and convicted the religious leaders for their complicity in the crime. It was common for wealthy landowners to rent their land to tenant farmers in return for a portion of the harvest. These landowners were notorious for treating their tenants harshly. Jesus turned the tables on this stereotypical scenario by depicting the tenants as the villains of his story.

After the tenant farmers mistreat the servants sent to collect the rent, the landowner decides to send his son. This is a clear allusion to Jesus as the unique Son of God sent by his Father, and as the fulfillment of the messianic promises made to King David. When the son arrives, the tenants wickedly realize this is their opportunity to usurp the inheritance of the son and take over the vineyard, so they decide to kill him. The detail of them taking him outside the walls of the vineyard prophetically pointed to Golgotha, the ominous rocky outcropping in an ancient stone quarry just outside the western walls of the city where the Romans carried out crucifixions.

Jesus then quoted Psalm 118: *"The stone that the builders rejected has become the cornerstone. This is what the Lord has done and it is wonderful in our eyes."* (Psalm 118:22-23) *"The builders"* is a clear reference to the religious leaders who would reject and condemn Jesus, turning him over to Pilate for crucifixion. *"The cornerstone"* is a clear reference to Jesus as the foundation of the new Kingdom he has begun to build through his church. Modern archaeology has demonstrated the rock of Golgotha was a section of the ancient limestone rock quarry not suitable for building, so the stone masons cut around it, leaving a 20-foot-tall outcropping. It is incredible to realize that Jesus was literally crucified on *"the stone that the builders rejected,"* just as he foretold!

Sadly, this meant the Jewish religious leaders would no longer be the primary stewards of God's Kingdom going forward. In a matter of 40 years, the Temple would be destroyed, the chief priests would be no more, and eventually the religious leaders would be driven from Jerusalem. A new people, a new family of God, made up of both Jews and Gentiles from every tribe and nation, would bring the Good News of God's Kingdom to the ends of the earth. The chief priests and Pharisees knew that Jesus was predicting their fate as well as his, but it only made them more determined to destroy him at any cost.

Have you ever been confronted by the consequences of your own disobedience? Did it cause you to repent or to deepen your determination to go your own way and not let anyone tell you what to do? The question is whether we will fall on the Stone and allow our stubborn self-will to be broken in repentance or will continue to resist God's purpose and be crushed under the stony weight of our disobedience. Lord, teach us to repent by listening to your Word and responding with steps of faith.

REFLECT AND RESPOND
What is Jesus saying to me right now?

What step of faith is Jesus calling me to take today?

DAY 57

READ AND LISTEN: MATTHEW 22:1-14
Take a minute to listen for what the Spirit is saying in these verses...

COMMENT AND CONSIDER
In the ancient Middle East, a wedding celebration was one of the most important events in the life of a family. You invited all your family, friends, and business contacts to as lavish a celebration as you could afford. There would be delicious food, fine wine, live music, and lots of dancing. In the case of a royal wedding, noble families from across the entire kingdom would be invited, and the celebration went on for days. An invitation to a royal wedding was one of the highest honors you could receive. Rejecting such an invitation, except for the most urgent reasons, would bring shame on you and your family.

Jesus continues his theme of rejection and judgment by telling a parable of a king who threw a great wedding banquet for his son. In the ancient world, you issued an advance invitation to let people know the day of the wedding celebration. Since people did not have clocks, it was common for a final notification to be delivered once everything was ready, indicating to the invited guests the time had come for the party to begin.

Jesus' story begins with this final notification as the servants *"summon those invited to the banquet."* However, one by one the invited guests said they were not coming without stating any reason at all. Instead of taking offense, the king sent his servants out a second time explaining the lavish meal was cooked and ready to eat, impressing on them both the incredible gift of the free banquet and the expense the host had paid to provide it. But inexplicably some of the invited guests simply wandered off to trivial tasks, while the rest beat and killed the king's servants. It is hard to imagine a more grievous offense in that culture!

Once the king's wrath was poured out on these traitorous subjects who reject his generosity, he decided to do something completely unexpected so the food didn't go to waste. This time he sent out his servants to *"invite everyone you find to the banquet."* This invitation was not based on social standing, economic status, or moral character. Everyone was invited without distinction to enjoy the bounty of the feast! But when a man was discovered at the banquet inappropriately dressed, he was thrown into the outer darkness. This is a reminder that, while the invitation is universal and free, there is only one way to enter the feast, through the righteousness of God that comes as a gift of grace. (See Isaiah 61:10; Matthew 5:20; Romans 3:21-26.)

Jesus concluded the parable by saying, *"For many are invited, but few are chosen."* The word translated *"many"* does not have a definite article, which means it is describing all, not just some. In the story everyone was invited, but only those who accepted the invitation and who entered on the king's terms were able to enjoy the feast. Jesus shows us how radically inclusive the Kingdom of God is, and yet that there is only one way to enter. As he said to his disciples, *"I am the way, the truth, and the life. No one comes to the Father except through me."* (John 14:6) The *"chosen"* in the Kingdom of God are those who accept the gift of grace by faith in Jesus and chose to follow him.

How have you responded to your King's invitation? Are you inviting everyone to join you in the banquet, so nothing goes to waste? Are you able to help others find the Way to enter the feast?

Reflect and Respond
What is Jesus saying to me right now?

What step of faith is Jesus calling me to take today?

DAY 58

READ AND LISTEN: MATTHEW 22:15-22
Take a minute to listen for what the Spirit is saying in these verses…

COMMENT AND CONSIDER
In the year 60 BC Julius Caesar was acclaimed Emperor by the Roman Senate, and so marked the end of the more democratic Roman Republic and the beginning of the more authoritarian Roman Empire. The nine Roman Emperors who followed Julius took his family name "Caesar" as their title. The Emperor at the time of Jesus' ministry was Tiberius Caesar, adopted son of Augustus Caesar, who ruled from AD 14-37. As the Roman Empire expanded, its strategy was to pacify the local populations they conquered, keep them as productive as possible, tax them as heavily as they could, and ship the profits back to the wealthy nobles in Rome.

The southern region of Israel was ruled directly by Roman governors like Pontius Pilate, but the northern regions were ruled on behalf of Rome by the sons of Herod the Great. Herod Antipas ruled Jesus' region of Galilee and collected taxes not only for Rome, but also to fund his ambitious building projects and lavish lifestyle. On top of this, the Jewish religious leaders also exacted taxes to support the Temple and religious institutions. Some scholars have estimated that Jews in Galilee at the time of Jesus paid up to 50% of their income in taxes each year.

The Herodians and the Pharisees were political enemies, but both were threatened by Jesus' authority and power. United by this common threat, they came to Jesus on the Temple Mount with a question designed to trap him in a self-incriminating statement. *"Is it lawful to pay taxes to Caesar or not?"* From Rome's point of view, any statement against paying taxes was considered treason, while the more zealous Jewish nationalists claimed paying taxes was collaborating with the enemy of Israel. No matter how Jesus answered, he would get in trouble with someone.

But Jesus' brilliant response transcended the politics of Palestine when he called for a silver coin and asked whose image and name it bore. They replied, *"Caesar's."* Herod Antipas had established a mint in his new capital city of Tiberius, and they stamped the image of Tiberius Caesar on the silver denarius coins there. And so Jesus said, *"Give, then, to Caesar the things that are Caesar's, and to God the things that are God's."* Jesus was alluding to the first chapter of Genesis which states that human beings are created in the image of God. While the silver coin bore the image of Tiberius, human beings bear in their inmost being the very image of God! Even those trying to trap Jesus were amazed and silenced by this profound answer.

Jesus pointed out that even though they needed to function as subjects of Rome and pay their taxes, their far higher allegiance was to the God in whose image they were created and to whom they were called to surrender everything, even their own lives. Jesus shows us that, as citizens of the kingdoms of this world, we are subject to human rulers, but our true citizenship is in the Kingdom of God. The kingdoms of this world are passing away, but the Kingdom of God is still coming and goes on forever. Following Jesus is how we learn to live according to the Kingdom of God today.

Are you a responsible citizen of your earthly kingdom? What does it mean to live as a faithful citizen of the Kingdom of heaven? Where does your ultimate allegiance lie? What does it look like for you to give to God the things that are God's?

Reflect and Respond

What is Jesus saying to me right now?

What step of faith is Jesus calling me to take today?

DAY 59

READ AND LISTEN: MATTHEW 22:23-33
Take a minute to listen for what the Spirit is saying in these verses…

COMMENT AND CONSIDER

The Sadducees and the Pharisees were the two leading Jewish religious groups at the time of Jesus. While the Pharisees were the teachers of the Law whose base of power was in the synagogue, the Sadducees came from the aristocratic priestly families of Jerusalem whose base of power was in the Temple. The Pharisees based their teaching on all the written books of the Hebrew Bible, as well as the interpretations of the rabbis which were passed down orally. The Sadducees, on the other hand, only taught the first five books of the Law and so didn't believe in angels, demons, or the resurrection, which only appear in the later books of the Old Testament.

Although these two groups had widely divergent political interests and theological viewpoints, they were united in their desire to negate the threat they perceived in Jesus. When the Herodians and Pharisees were not able to trap Jesus with their trick question, the Sadducees decided to take their turn. They posed a complicated scenario in which a series of brothers died childless in an attempt to refute Jesus' teaching of the resurrection of the dead.

In Deuteronomy 25:5-10, the Law states that if a man dies without an heir, his brother is to marry the widowed sister-in-law to provide for her and to continue his brother's line of descendants. The Sadducees posited a situation in which seven brothers died, each marrying the same sister-in-law. The question they posed to Jesus was, when this woman died, *In the resurrection, then, whose wife will she be of the seven?* By creating this conundrum, they were trying to discredit the teaching of the resurrection of the dead.

Again, Jesus' response transcended the question itself. He said that *"in the resurrection they neither marry nor are given in marriage but are like angels in heaven."* His point is that marriage does not apply in the fully realized Kingdom of

God after we are raised from the dead. Then he went on to show that the resurrection is confirmed by God's statement, *"I am the God of Abraham and the God of Isaac and the God of Jacob."* The present tense of this divine declaration demonstrates that the patriarchs, though long dead from our point of view, are fully alive in the presence of God.

Jesus' indictment of the Sadducees was not just in his ability to refute their question, but even more in his statement, *"You are mistaken, because you don't know the Scriptures or the power of God."* Their mistake was not recognizing the inspiration of the entire Hebrew Bible and not allowing God's Word to create faith in their hearts. (See Romans 10:17.) When we are seeking to understand God's Word, it is critical that we read each passage in the wider context of the entire Bible. It is also critical that we allow the Holy Spirit to guide us into all the truth, asking him to speak faith into our hearts through his Word. This is how God's Word becomes *"living and effective and sharper than any double-edged sword."* (Hebrews 4:12)

How are you using the Bible in your life? Is reading God's Word producing faith in your heart? How can you invite the Holy Spirit to guide your understanding of Scripture so you can respond with informed steps of faith?

Reflect and Respond

What is Jesus saying to me right now?

What step of faith is Jesus calling me to take today?

DAY 60

READ AND LISTEN: MATTHEW 22:34-40
Take a minute to listen for what the Spirit is saying in these verses…

COMMENT AND CONSIDER
After being thwarted in their attempts to trap Jesus, the religious leaders came up with one more try. *"Teacher, which command in the law is the greatest?"* There was an ongoing debate among the rabbis about which of the 613 identified laws of the Hebrew Bible was the most important. The Ten Commandments are an obvious top ten list, but was it possible to narrow the field even further? Jesus' reply brilliantly sums up the entire intent of all the commands by connecting our vertical relationship with our horizontal relationships.

In the time of Jesus, faithful Jews recited memorized prayers three times a day. The famous "Shema" from Deuteronomy was part of the morning and evening prayers, *"Listen, Israel: The Lord our God, the Lord is one. Love the Lord your God with all your heart, with all your soul, and with all your strength."* (Deuteronomy 6:4-5) These words were etched in the consciousness of Jesus' listeners through repetition. Jesus' profound insight was to lift this foundational aspect of our relationship with God out of the thick forest of commandments that so easily crowd out what is most important: receiving God's love and reciprocating that love. Loving God with all that we are is the most important thing.

First-century rabbis often strung together various passages of Scripture by connecting them with the theme of a common word. Jesus does exactly that by connecting the Shema from Deuteronomy with a passage in Leviticus based on the common theme of love. *"Do not take revenge or bear a grudge against members of your community, but love your neighbor as yourself; I am the Lord."* (Leviticus 19:18) Jesus shows us the critical connection between our relationship with God and our relationship with each other. When we receive and reciprocate the unconditional love that God pours into our hearts through the Holy Spirit (see Romans 5:5), that love can then overflow in unconditional love for those around us. Jesus says this is the other most important thing.

Love is the deliberate choice to seek what is good for another, even if it requires sacrifice. To love God is to seek what is good for him. Of course, God is perfect and needs nothing from us. All God wants is for us to love him and live in harmony with his good purpose. That is why loving God is synonymous with doing his will. True obedience does not come from a slavish attempt to follow religious rules but is the natural outcome of loving God. As John says, *"For this is what love for God is: to keep his commands. And his commands are not a burden."* (1 John 5:3)

Likewise, loving our neighbor means seeking what is best for others, even if it means giving up what we want. Jesus said, *"No one has greater love than this: to lay down his life for his friends."* (John 15:13) How do we find the strength to love in this way? It is from the overflow of our relationship with God. As John says, *"Love consists in this: not that we loved God, but that he loved us and sent his Son to be the atoning sacrifice for our sins. Dear friends, if God loved us in this way, we also must love one another… We love because he first loved us."* (1 John 4:10-11, 19)

How can you receive God's love more fully today? How can you express your love for God more consistently? How can the love you share with God empower you to love those around you sacrificially?

REFLECT AND RESPOND
What is Jesus saying to me right now?

What step of faith is Jesus calling me to take today?

Footsteps Every Week: Review

Write a brief summary of what Jesus said to you each day this past week and the step of faith he called you to take:

Monday

Tuesday

Wednesday

Thursday

Friday

Saturday

Footsteps Every Week: Reflect

Big Picture

As you look over what Jesus has said to you this past week, do you see any themes? What is the most important thing you need to remember and believe?

Predictable Pattern

As you look over what Jesus called you to do this past week, is there a new predictable pattern he is inviting you to establish in your life with God and others?

Plant the Word

As you look over the readings from this past week, write out the passage that feels most important for you and memorize it over the next week:

DAY 61

READ AND LISTEN: MATTHEW 22:41-46
Take a minute to listen for what the Spirit is saying in these verses…

COMMENT AND CONSIDER
Jesus spoke with an unprecedented authority as a direct representative of his Father and demonstrated supernatural power in his ministry of healing and deliverance. This threatened the religious leaders' power base, and they were ready to do whatever it took to eliminate him. All day long on the Temple Mount, the religious leaders had tried to trap Jesus with trick questions, baiting him to say something to give them an excuse to arrest him. Now Jesus turned the tables by asking them a loaded question.

The big question Jesus' actions provoked throughout his ministry was whether he was the long-awaited Messiah who would fulfill God's promise to raise up a king to establish an eternal kingdom of justice and peace for his people. The prophet Nathan spoke God's promise to David, *"When your time comes and you rest with your ancestors, I will raise up after you your descendant, who will come from your body, and I will establish… the throne of his kingdom forever. I will be his father, and he will be my son."* (2 Samuel 7:12-14)

David's son Solomon built the first Temple in Jerusalem, but he did not fulfill God's promise to vanquish Israel's enemies, establish them in the land, and bring an eternal kingdom of peace. And so the people of Israel continued to look for the promised descendant of David who would rule over an eternal kingdom. Jesus was a descendant of David and did the very things the prophets foretold the Messiah would do, such as bringing good news to the poor, healing the brokenhearted, and proclaiming liberty to the captives. (See Isaiah 61:1.) So it was not surprising that many wondered if he was their long-awaited King, the Son of David. The blind men in Jericho certainly thought so, and once Jesus made his symbolic entrance into Jerusalem even the children in the Temple were identifying him as the Son of David!

It is in this context that Jesus turned the tables on the Pharisees, the biblical scholars of the day, asking them why David began his famous messianic Psalm 110 by writing, *"This is the declaration of the L*ORD *to my Lord."* He then went on to describe how the Messiah King would defeat the enemies of Israel. David called the Messiah "Lord," and Jesus pointed out how this makes no sense if the Messiah is merely a human descendant of David. Why would the father call his son "Lord" unless this descendant was more than just his biological offspring?

The religious leaders were not able to answer without conceding that the Messiah was, in fact, a divine King who would truly rule forever, and so they refused to answer. John recorded another confrontation between Jesus and his detractors on the Temple Mount when Jesus said, *"Truly I tell you, before Abraham was, I am."* When they heard this, the people picked up stones to throw at him because they understood he was claiming to be divine. (See John 8:57-59.) Many people think of Jesus as nothing more than a great human teacher, but Jesus himself claimed divinity and accepted the worship of his followers who, particularly after his resurrection from the dead, recognized him as the incarnate Son of God, fully divine.

How do you see Jesus? Do you recognize that in his full humanity he has given you an example to follow in everything he did? Do you recognize that in his full divinity he has the power to save you, transform you, and fulfill all his promises? This is the Jesus we follow and worship.

Reflect and Respond
What is Jesus saying to me right now?

What step of faith is Jesus calling me to take today?

DAY 62

READ AND LISTEN: MATTHEW 23:1-12
Take a minute to listen for what the Spirit is saying in these verses…

COMMENT AND CONSIDER
The scribes were trained experts in the Law who taught in the synagogue prayer services on the Sabbath day and taught the boys in the synagogue school during the week. The Pharisees were the elite scribes who claimed an even more zealous devotion to the Law, not only the written Law of the Old Testament, but even more the oral law, which was comprised of the interpretations of various rabbis, passed down from generation to generation. The oral law was an attempt to apply the Law to contemporary life and was seen as a fence built around the written Law to make sure no one got close to breaking the commandments of God. The Pharisees believed the oral law had been passed down from the time of Moses and considered it to be equally as binding as the written Law.

A special seat at the front of the synagogue called the "Moses Seat" was designated for the teacher to sit in while he taught the people. Jesus affirmed the role of those who taught the Law of Moses, *"those who sit in Moses' seat,"* but he did not recognize the authority of the religious traditions handed down by the rabbis.

The problem with the oral law was that it continued to grow and become more and more complex, with new rules and rituals added in each successive generation. Jesus described this legalistic system as a huge burden piled on the backs of everyday people by the religious elite who did not even follow the spirit of their own teachings, much less the Law of Moses. Instead, they did things motivated by the status it conferred upon them and the public approval it generated. Jesus was criticizing the hierarchical system they created which elevated the leaders over the rest of the people.

A phylactery (Hebrew: *tefillin*) is a small leather box containing a tiny scroll with four verses from the Hebrew Scriptures written on them. (See Exodus

13:9, 16; Deuteronomy 6:8; 11:18.) This box was connected to a leather strap wrapped around the forearm or strapped to the forehead in literal obedience of Deuteronomy 11:18. Four tassels were attached to the four corners of men's garments *"to look at and remember all the commandments of the Lord."* (See Numbers 15:37–41.) Jesus was not rejecting these practices but criticized those who exaggerated the importance of these items to impress others.

The seats closest to the host at a banquet were considered the places of honor, with a descending level of importance the further from the host you sat. Similarly, special seats of prominence in the front of the synagogue facing the rest of the congregation were reserved for the synagogue leaders. Titles such as "rabbi," "father," and "instructor" brought status and power to those who claimed them. Again, Jesus was not necessarily rejecting these titles—people often addressed him as "Rabbi"—but was rather criticizing the lording of these titles over others to gain status and power.

In contrast to these leaders who placed themselves above others, Jesus demonstrated genuine humility by lifting up the oppressed, welcoming the outcast, and washing his disciples' feet. As he said, *"the Son of Man did not come to be served, but to serve, and to give his life as a ransom for many."* (Matthew 20:28) He reminded us *"you are all brothers and sisters."* What are the ways you subtly try to use religion to put yourself above others? What does it mean to treat each other as brothers and sisters in the family of God?

Reflect and Respond
What is Jesus saying to me right now?

What step of faith is Jesus calling me to take today?

DAY 63

READ AND LISTEN: MATTHEW 23:13-22
Take a minute to listen for what the Spirit is saying in these verses…

COMMENT AND CONSIDER
Jesus continued his criticism of the religious leaders with a series of seven *"woes."* Old Testament prophets sometimes pronounced God's judgment by beginning *"Woe to you…"* and then naming the cause of their judgment. (For example, see Isaiah 3:9-11.) Six of Jesus' seven indictments of these leaders begin, *"Woe to you, scribes and Pharisees, hypocrites!"*

Just a few miles from Jesus' hometown of Nazareth stood the large, Roman-style city of Sepphoris, built by Herod Antipas as the capital of Galilee. Jesus grew up in a family of builders who would have been involved in the construction of that city, with Jesus himself working there from the age of 12 to 30. One of the prominent features of Sepphoris was a large theater built into the hillside where actors put on Greek plays, among other performances. Jesus applies the same term to the Pharisees that was used to describe actors who wore masks in the Greek theater: *"hypocrites!"* They were pretenders. As Jesus said earlier, *"they don't practice what they teach."* (Matthew 23:3)

Jesus' first indictment of these leaders is that they *"shut the door of the kingdom of heaven in people's faces."* As we have seen, the Kingdom of Heaven is the central theme of Jesus' teaching in which he describes this movement of God to bring heaven to earth by empowering us to do his will on earth as it is in heaven. Ironically, even though the scribes and Pharisees were obsessed with doing the will of God as revealed in the Law, their legalism accomplished exactly the opposite. They failed to participate in God's Kingdom and kept others from living in that reality as well.

Jesus' second indictment is that the leaders make converts who become *"twice as much a child of hell as you are!"* Discipleship is the process of communicating information and offering a model to imitate. Inevitably we reproduce what we are. In the case of the scribes and Pharisees, they multiplied in others the same dysfunction that plagued their own self-serving, self-righteous way of life. This is what Jesus refers to as a bad tree producing bad fruit. (See Matthew 7:17-18.)

Jesus' third indictment of these leaders is that they are *"blind guides,"* an ironic image to be sure! To illustrate, he pointed to their complex series of legal rulings which distinguished between oaths made *"by the temple"* and those made *"by the gold of the temple,"* the latter being more binding. This was an example of how they valued the religious systems they had created over the revealed will of God himself. Idolatry is when we treat anything as more important than God. This is simply the blind leading the blind.

Some of us are in official positions of leadership and are responsible for the teaching and spiritual guidance of others in our community. We need to take special notice of these "woes" to make sure we don't fall into the same traps as the scribes and Pharisees. But the rest of us who are not in official roles of spiritual leadership would do well to recognize that we are all leaders to someone, whether we realize it. Our attitudes and our actions represent Jesus everywhere we go, either for good or for bad, and we are all accountable for that influence.

What "woe" is Jesus warning you about? Are you slamming the door to the Kingdom or making children of hell without realizing it? How can you learn to live as a person of integrity rather than a hypocrite?

Reflect and Respond

What is Jesus saying to me right now?

What step of faith is Jesus calling me to take today?

DAY 64

READ AND LISTEN: MATTHEW 23:23-32

Take a minute to listen for what the Spirit is saying in these verses...

COMMENT AND CONSIDER

In the Old Testament Law, God commands the people of Israel to give back a tithe from their income. *"Every tenth of the land's produce, grain from the soil or fruit from the trees, belongs to the Lord; it is holy to the Lord."* (Leviticus 27:30) The Pharisees measured out tiny amounts of mint, dill, and cumin from their herb gardens in order make sure they did not break this 10% rule, even though these spices were of negligible value. In the next "woe," Jesus wasn't criticizing their attention to detail, but he pointed out how much less significant that law is than the more important ethical calling of God to live according to his justice, mercy, and faithfulness—something they were neglecting. As the prophet Micah said, *"Mankind, he has told each of you what is good and what it is the Lord requires of you: to act justly, to love faithfulness, and to walk humbly with your God."* (Micah 6:8)

The Law specifies which kind of winged insects are considered clean to eat and then says, *"All other winged insects that have four feet are to be abhorrent to you."* (Leviticus 11:23) For this reason Pharisees carefully strained their wine before drinking it so they did not inadvertently swallow a gnat or other tiny unclean insect. Jesus described their obsession with symbolic rituals and their avoidance of important ethical concerns, using the image of straining out a gnat while swallowing a camel! This is what happens when we major in the minors, rather than keeping perspective on what really matters in the Kingdom of God.

The next two woes illustrate the futility of an externally focused religion that fails to address the inner life of a person. Great effort went into making sure the dishes people used for their meals were ritually pure, so that the dishes didn't make their food impure. Since the Jews considered dead bodies ritually impure, they painted whitewash on tombs to make sure no one inadvertently stepped on a grave and accidentally became ceremonially unclean. Both of these traditions offer a vivid picture of how pointless the Pharisees' emphasis on outward obedience was, since they did not address the attitudes and motivations that shape a person's heart and soul.

Many impressive monumental tombs were carved from the living rock in the Kidron Valley between Jerusalem and the Mount of Olives, and some still stand today. Many prophets and other esteemed religious leaders were buried on the slopes of the Mount of Olives. In the time of Jesus, these tombs of the famous were lavishly decorated, even if the leaders had been rejected and executed by the establishment in their own time. In this seventh woe, Jesus called out the hypocrisy of those who gave lip service to honoring these prophets when they did not live by the challenging message that got the prophets killed in the first place. It is a little like people today who quote civil rights leaders like Dr. Martin Luther King Jr., after they have become widely revered, but demonstrate by their actions that they would not have embraced the message of these leaders when they were alive.

Do you have perspective on what is really important in God's Kingdom, or have you focused on things that are relatively unimportant? Are you attending to the spiritual condition of your inner self so that what you express outwardly is truly good fruit that will last? Are you giving lip service to politically correct values, or do you really live according to the prophets that you honor?

Reflect and Respond
What is Jesus saying to me right now?

What step of faith is Jesus calling me to take today?

DAY 65

READ AND LISTEN: MATTHEW 23:33-39
Take a minute to listen for what the Spirit is saying in these verses…

COMMENT AND CONSIDER
Jesus concluded his diatribe against the religious leaders of Jerusalem with harsh language reminiscent of his cousin John the Baptist, who also called out the hypocrisy of religious leaders by comparing them to *"a brood of vipers."* (Mathew 3:7) Jesus explained that, down through the ages, God sent prophets to his people to point out the error of their ways and save them from the consequences of their mistakes. However, too often the response to this loving correction was not repentance, but resistance and rebellion.

We can see in Scripture a troubling pattern of powerful rulers killing prophets who dare to challenge their corruption. King Ahab and his Phoenician Queen Jezebel slaughtered all the prophets of God who dared to question their embrace of pagan worship and immorality, except for Elijah, whom they could never quite get their hands on. (See 1 Kings 18:4; 19:10.) The final Jewish prophet whose martyrdom is recorded in Scripture was Zechariah, son of the high priest Jehoiada. (See 2 Chronicles 24:20-21.) At the time of Jesus, a book called "The Lives of the Prophets" told the story of the other prophets who were brutally killed for their message, such as Isaiah, Jeremiah, Ezekiel, Micah, and Amos. Jesus summarized this long, violent history of martyrdom when he referred to *"the righteous blood shed on the earth"* from Abel to Zechariah.

Jesus had already foretold his impending execution numerous times, not only to his closest disciples, but also to the crowds in the parable of the landowner and the tenants. (See Matthew 21:33-46.) It seems certain the painful memory of his cousin John's recent murder at the hands of Herod Antipas weighed heavily on him when he prophesied that many more *"prophets, sages, and scribes"* who followed in his footsteps were sure to meet the same fate. Some would be beaten and persecuted, others would be killed. In fact, it wasn't long before Jesus' follower Stephen was stoned outside the walls of Jerusalem by the religious leaders. (See Acts 7:58-59.) After that, one of the twelve disciples, James, the son of Zebedee, was beheaded by Herod Agrippa. (Acts 12:1-2) Historical tradition tells us eventually eleven of the twelve original disciples were killed for their testimony of what Jesus had done in their lives.

In the face of this evil brutality, Jesus cried out to the very people of Jerusalem who had and were about to carry out these atrocities. He offered the tender image of a mother hen gathering her chicks under her wings for protection and invited them to come under his protection. Sadly, Jesus knew the majority of the people would not come to him but would face the judgment of their own rebellion. Although he entered Jerusalem to the messianic chant from Psalm 118, *"Blessed is he who comes in the name of the Lord,"* Jesus knew the chants would soon change to *"Crucify him!"* And while he would rise from the dead, Jerusalem and the Temple would soon lie in smoldering ruins.

Who are the prophets in our lives today? Do we give them respect and listen to their message? How do we respond when confronted with our own unintentional mistakes and even our willful rebellion? Do we humble ourselves and allow God to change our minds, or do we dig in with stubborn resistance and try to justify our mistakes and inaction? Jesus invites us to draw near to him and find shelter under the protection of his loving wings. Or we can ignore him and go our own way, which inevitably leads to destruction.

Who loves you enough to speak the truth to you? Are you listening to them? How are you responding? Jesus' call is *"repent and believe."* Those are the two questions with which we conclude every daily devotion. Repent: Jesus, what are you saying to me? Believe: What is the step of faith you are calling me to take right now? Will you resist and rebel, or repent and believe?

Reflect and Respond
What is Jesus saying to me right now?

What step of faith is Jesus calling me to take today?

DAY 66

READ AND LISTEN: MATTHEW 24:1-28
Take a minute to listen for what the Spirit is saying in these verses…

COMMENT AND CONSIDER
In 20 BC Herod the Great tried to gain favor with the people by launching an ambitious renovation of the Temple. He built massive retaining walls using enormous stone blocks which allowed him to expand the courtyard around the Temple to its current size, equal to 25 American football fields. In AD 70, following the first Jewish revolt, the Romans wiped out every building on the Temple Mount, but could not tear down the massive platform on which they were built. When you visit Jerusalem today, you can still see the huge blocks of limestone Herod's builders cut to hold up the platform. In fact, one forty-foot-long stone in the western wall weighs more than 600 tons! It is no wonder the disciples who came from rural Galilee were awestruck by the sheer size, not to mention the architectural beauty, of this amazing complex.

One day, when Jesus and his disciples were coming down from the Temple complex, the disciples were expressing their awe, but Jesus said, *"Do you see all these things? Truly I tell you, not one stone will be left here on another that will not be thrown down."* They must have walked on in shocked silence wondering what it would take to bring down these massive structures and how Jesus would know such a thing. Once they had crossed the Kidron Valley and sat alone with Jesus up on the Mount of Olives, they got a view of the entire Temple Mount. They must have thought this magnificent structure would last until the end of time, and so they began asking their Rabbi about *"the end of the age."*

Jesus began by warning them of false prophets and messiahs who would come to deceive them and lead them astray. Messianic pretenders were not unusual in first-century Palestine. Judas the Galilean raised a messianic movement during Jesus' childhood, and Simon Bar Kokhba was the messianic leader of the second Jewish revolt about a hundred years after Jesus' resurrection. Jesus said to be skeptical of such charismatic leaders, even of those who come in his name. He also cautioned them not to assign too much meaning to the outbreak of war and natural disasters like famines and earthquakes because these are just *"the beginning of labor pains."*

Jesus warned times of persecution were coming. However, the word which is translated in v. 9 *"persecuted"* (Greek: *thylpsis*) refers to a period of tribulation or distress for people in general. Jesus was prophesying the destruction that would befall the people of Jerusalem some 40 years later, when the Romans laid siege to the city and burned it to the ground. But there was a secondary meaning, looking far into the future, when the end of time arrives, the great and final conflict between good and evil finally comes to a head, and the Son of Man returns.

About this dramatic conclusion to history, Jesus said, *"This good news of the kingdom will be proclaimed in all the world as a testimony to all nations, and then the end will come."* This is a reminder that our job is to proclaim and embody the Good News of the Kingdom no matter what. We aren't responsible for the timing or the details of the end times; that is in God's hands. Jesus said our job through all these tumultuous times is to endure and be people of Good News.

What is Jesus calling you to endure today? How can you be and share Good News in the midst of it all?

Reflect and Respond
What is Jesus saying to me right now?

What step of faith is Jesus calling me to take today?

Footsteps Every Week: Review

Write a brief summary of what Jesus said to you each day this past week and the step of faith he called you to take:

Monday

Tuesday

Wednesday

Thursday

Friday

Saturday

Footsteps Every Week: Reflect

Big Picture

As you look over what Jesus has said to you this past week, do you see any themes? What is the most important thing you need to remember and believe?

Predictable Pattern

As you look over what Jesus called you to do this past week, is there a new predictable pattern he is inviting you to establish in your life with God and others?

Plant the Word

As you look over the readings from this past week, write out the passage that feels most important for you and memorize it over the next week:

DAY 67

READ AND LISTEN: MATTHEW 24:29-35
Take a minute to listen for what the Spirit is saying in these verses…

COMMENT AND CONSIDER
Biblical prophecy is filled with layers of meaning. Often there is a more immediate historical meaning that can be applied in the near-term, and a secondary, longer-term meaning is layered beneath it. Most of the messianic prophecies of the Old Testament foretell the coming of the Messiah along with cataclysmic events. At first reading we might assume the coming of the Messiah and these events are one and the same, but on closer examination we see that these are two different historical layers of meaning. Discerning the difference between these two layers is critical to our understanding of biblical prophecy.

Jesus' first coming in his full humanity launched an invisible Kingdom inaugurated by his unique way of life, his revelatory teaching, his sacrificial death on the cross, and his glorious resurrection from the dead. This Kingdom continued to grow through the outpouring of his Spirit into the lives of those who followed in his footsteps and represented his Way by making disciples who could make disciples and proclaiming the Good News of the Kingdom. Jesus warned they would face a period of intense upheaval and uncertainty in the near future. This is the first layer of meaning in Jesus' prophecy.

However, a second layer has a much longer time horizon. Jesus prophesied that one day he will return in the fullness of his unmistakable divine glory to bring the story of human redemption to a dramatic conclusion through earth-shaking events. His glorious return will once and for all wipe out sin, death, hell, and the devil and fully establish God's rule on earth as it is in heaven. Jesus will come *"on the clouds of heaven with power and great glory,"* appearing to everyone on earth in such a way that no one can ignore or avoid him. In this cataclysmic moment, God will gather his people together *"from the four winds of the earth,"* meaning those who have died and those who are still alive will be brought together in one cosmic family reunion to be established forever as God's people in a new heaven and a new earth.

It is hard to comprehend how terrifying this will be for those who persist in their stubborn rebellion against God and how wonderful it will be for those who embrace his Son Jesus! In his first coming, Jesus lived a mostly inauspicious life. Only those who open their hearts to this Messiah and receive his love and grace will recognize his true glory and majesty. But when Jesus returns, the true scope of his power and glory will be made evident to every person, living and dead. There will be no mistaking who he is and why he has come. As the ancient creed quoted by Paul says, in that day *"every knee will bow— in heaven and on earth and under the earth— and every tongue will confess that Jesus Christ is Lord, to the glory of God the Father."* (Philippians 2:10-11)

If you are in a relationship with Jesus and are following him by faith, you are already part of his eternal family and will continue participating in his glorious Kingdom for all of eternity! This is the goal toward which human history is inevitably moving. This is the eternal destiny of all those who trust and follow Jesus. How does knowing this affect you in the humdrum routines of day to day living? How does this help you persevere in the face of your daily challenges?

Reflect and Respond
What is Jesus saying to me right now?

What step of faith is Jesus calling me to take today?

DAY 68

READ AND LISTEN: MATTHEW 24:36-44
Take a minute to listen for what the Spirit is saying in these verses…

COMMENT AND CONSIDER
The disciples were still sitting with Jesus on the Mount of Olives looking out over Jerusalem when he finally answered their question, *"Tell us, when will these things happen?"* (Matthew 24:3) This is the question everyone asks still today when they hear Jesus' teaching on the end times! When will Jesus come back? When will the end of the world come?

Jesus' answer is shocking. He said he doesn't know! Angels don't know the timing. The Son of God doesn't know the timing. Only God the Father knows the day and the hour of Jesus' return. When you hear self-styled prophets predicting details about when Jesus will return, just remember they are claiming to know more than Jesus.

Jesus' admission that he doesn't know is a reminder that God emptied himself when he took on human flesh and chose to operate in his full humanity during the 33 or so years Jesus lived on earth. Jesus exercised neither omniscience nor omnipotence during his earthly life. He didn't know everything, and in his own power he was not able to do anything he wanted. He operated in the supernatural power of the Spirit to do God's will and was able to prophetically know things that were beyond human knowledge, but he did these things by faith. Jesus set an example for us to follow so we could learn to live in the supernatural power of the Spirit as he did.

Jesus told his disciples they could look for the signs of his coming, but they should not get too concerned over the normal, destabilizing events of human history like war, famine, and earthquakes. (See Matthew 24:6-8.) However, he tells us that when we see unprecedented events beginning to take place in the sky, it is our clue the end is near, just as the buds on a fig tree tell you summer is about to arrive. Jesus compared us to the people in

Noah's day. Noah didn't know exactly when the flood would come; he just knew it was coming and so was obedient to prepare.

Jesus illustrated how sudden his return will be by depicting people going about their ordinary, everyday tasks, when suddenly they are either included in the consummated Kingdom of God (*"taken"*) or relegated to the cataclysmic judgment coming on all of the darkness in this world (*"left"*). This is the first of a series of images Jesus used to teach us what it means to be alert and ready for his return, even though we don't know the day or the hour. The first of these images is a thief breaking into a house. A thief would never let us know when he was planning to break in! We have to be alert and ready if we want to thwart the thief. In the same way, Jesus said, we need to live with a constant awareness that our time in this broken world is limited and he is coming back.

The Apostle Paul seemed to comment on these very teachings of Jesus when he wrote to the followers of Jesus in Thessalonica, *"About the times and the seasons: Brothers and sisters, you do not need anything to be written to you. For you yourselves know very well that the day of the Lord will come just like a thief in the night… So then, let us not sleep, like the rest, but let us stay awake and be self-controlled."* (1 Thessalonians 5:1-2, 6)

How does knowing Jesus will return change the way you are living? How can you be prepared even though you don't know when it will happen?

Reflect and Respond
What is Jesus saying to me right now?

What step of faith is Jesus calling me to take today?

DAY 69

READ AND LISTEN: MATTHEW 24:45-51
Take a minute to listen for what the Spirit is saying in these verses…

COMMENT AND CONSIDER
In biblical times people lived in extended families made up of multiple generations of biological family as well as friends, business partners, and slaves. The Greek word for this kind of family and the compound where they lived is *oikos*. A wealthy *oikos* would include a number of slaves who carried out duties ranging from menial tasks to complex business transactions. The head slave of a household like this was called the *oikonomos*, which literally means "the ruler of the *oikos*." This word is often translated "steward" or "manager."

An *oikonomos* of a wealthy family was a person of considerable social status and power because they typically ran the family business, oversaw all the other slaves and employees of the family, and often managed the family's personal affairs as well. A competent and trustworthy *oikonomos* was highly valued because it allowed the master to travel and live a life free of concern for the daily affairs of the family and the family business.

To explain what it means to be prepared for his return, Jesus told a parable about a faithful and wise slave who was put in charge of managing the family's meals while his master was away. That slave had no way of knowing when his master would return, but when he did return, the master found that slave was responsibly and competently purchasing groceries, planning menus, and preparing meals to feed the family. He was so pleased with this slave that he promoted him to the position of *oikonomos* and put him in charge of the entire household. On the other hand, if the master returns unexpectedly and discovers this slave mistreating the slaves he was responsible for and stealing the family's food and wine to feast and get drunk with his degenerate friends, the master's response will be very different. This slave's punishment will include being banished to a place of weeping and teeth-grinding along with the hypocrites, such as the scribes and Pharisees, whom Jesus had warned earlier.

Being prepared for Jesus' return means functioning as wise and faithful slaves who don't have to worry about when the master is coming back because we are focused on the tasks we have been assigned. If we are faithful stewards of the role we have been given, God will entrust even greater responsibility to us because we have proven to be trustworthy.

I invite you to put yourself in this story and ask, do I consider myself a slave in my Father's household? If so, what are the tasks I have been assigned? What does it mean for me to be wise and faithful in these tasks? Am I faithful and true to my calling even when it seems no one is looking?

REFLECT AND RESPOND

What is Jesus saying to me right now?

What step of faith is Jesus calling me to take today?

DAY 70

READ AND LISTEN: MATTHEW 25:1-13
Take a minute to listen for what the Spirit is saying in these verses…

COMMENT AND CONSIDER
In biblical times the typical wedding was conducted at the bride's family home. After the ceremony, the groom and his closest friends joyfully wound their way through the village, leading the bride on a donkey to the groom's home where the rest of the family and friends were waiting to welcome the bride into her new extended family. The joyful procession took the longest route in order to pass as many houses as possible to receive the congratulations of the entire village. The guests waiting at the groom's family home had no idea exactly when the wedding party would arrive, except that it would probably be after dark.

Jesus tells this parable about ten of the bride's unmarried friends who are waiting at the groom's family home to welcome their friend and her new husband. The word translated *"lamp"* in this story is not the small, clay lamps that were used indoors, but rather a larger kind of lamp, more like a torch, which would not be extinguished by the wind. In traditional Middle Eastern culture, it was considered inappropriate for a woman to be out in public without a lamp. The assumption was that if a woman is lurking in the dark, she has something to hide and so must be up to no good. Also, it was safer for a woman to have a lamp at night so she was less likely to be attacked in the dark where no one could see her attacker.

So each of these young women had their own outdoor lamp shining brightly. As should have been expected, the night was dragging on, the wedding party had not arrived, and all ten of the young women nodded off to sleep. Five of them were wise enough to anticipate this inevitable delay and planned accordingly by bringing their extra flasks of oil to replenish the lamps. However, five of them were foolish and didn't bring any extra oil. Suddenly they were roused from slumber by the joyful shouts of the approaching wedding party!

The five foolish girls suddenly realized their lamps were about to go out because they had burned all their oil. Since the other five did not have oil to spare, the five foolish women were forced to go search for oil and completely missed the arrival of their friend and her new husband. To make matters worse, when they did return to the house, the outer door was securely locked and they were turned away because the master of the banquet said, *"I don't know you."*

Jesus is giving us a picture of what it means to plan ahead and be ready to participate in his coming Kingdom. Most of the early disciples assumed Jesus would return very quickly, maybe just a few years after his ascension into heaven. Which of them could have imagined we would be reading this parable some 2000 years later, still trying to learn how to prepare for the arrival of our bridegroom Jesus? Participating in God's coming Kingdom is a marathon, not a sprint, and we need to train for the long haul.

Another lesson is that we each have a responsibility for our own personal preparation. We can't assume we can borrow oil from someone else when Jesus shows up later than we assumed. We all have to stand before Jesus and give an account for how we have responded to his call to follow him into God's Kingdom.

Are you preparing for a spiritual sprint or a marathon? Are you relying on the faith of others or is your faith truly your own?

Reflect and Respond
What is Jesus saying to me right now?

What step of faith is Jesus calling me to take today?

DAY 71

READ AND LISTEN: MATTHEW 25:14-30
Take a minute to listen for what the Spirit is saying in these verses...

COMMENT AND CONSIDER

It was not uncommon for a wealthy landowner to go on a long journey and entrust his property to slaves while he was gone. In this parable Jesus depicts a wealthy individual who entrusts his wealth to three of his slaves. A *"talent"* was not a coin but a monetary unit. In this case they were talents of silver, each of which weighed about 75 pounds, equaling 6,000 denarii. In today's money that would be about $250,000 USD, but in practical terms it would have been even more valuable because the average worker in first-century Palestine made so much less than most of us do today.

The master entrusts $1.25 million to the first slave, half a million to the second, and a quarter of a million to the third. His distribution of the money is based on *"each one's ability."* The first slave immediately put the money to work, which means he engaged in some kind of commercial activity. It could mean he bought local goods, had them shipped somewhere else, and sold them at a profit. The point is he invested the money in practical business that earned a good return, and he doubled his master's capital for a total of $2.5 million!

The second slave did the same and doubled his half a million doing business, for a total of $1 million! Both these slaves trusted their master enough to take the risk of doing business with his money. Both these slaves were praised by the master for putting his money to work and earning a good return. Both these slaves were promised greater opportunities because they proved their faithfulness, and both were invited to share in the joy they had brought to their master. It didn't seem to matter to the master that one had earned over a million more in profit than the other; all he cared about was that they put the capital to work according to their ability.

The third slave had a completely different perspective on his master. He was afraid of the master, believing he was a harsh man who took what wasn't his. All the evidence in the story tells us this slave misunderstood his master. As a result, he acted in fear rather than faith, and hid the master's money in the ground where it could earn no return. There were no banks in first-century Jewish society where you could deposit your money for safe-keeping and earn a little interest, but you could lend your money to a moneychanger who would pay a small percentage of the profits he earned from it.

When the master saw that the third slave had acted in fear and done nothing profitable with his money, not even lending it to a moneychanger, he stripped him of all his capital, gave it to the first slave who now had eleven talents, and consigned him to outer darkness. His assessment of the third slave was that he was evil and lazy because he acted in fear rather than faith and did nothing with the huge gift that was entrusted to him.

To prepare for Jesus' coming and participate in his Kingdom is to do business with the many capitals he has entrusted to us. It is not about how much he has entrusted to us; it is about what we do with what he has placed in our hands. Are you afraid of failure? Do you see God as a harsh master or a master who is helping you to multiply what he has entrusted to you?

Reflect and Respond

What is Jesus saying to me right now?

What step of faith is Jesus calling me to take today?

DAY 72

READ AND LISTEN: MATTHEW 25:31-46

Take a minute to listen for what the Spirit is saying in these verses…

COMMENT AND CONSIDER

Jesus told four parables illustrating how we are to prepare for the end of the world, and now he describes the final judgment. The Prophet Daniel foretold that *"one like a son of man"* would descend from heaven to earth where he will receive an eternal Kingdom from the Ancient of Days. (See Daniel 7:9-14.) This divine human will join the Ancient of Days at the final judgment when *"Many who sleep in the dust of the earth will awake, some to eternal life, and some to disgrace and eternal contempt."* (Daniel 12:2)

Jesus uses the phrase *"Son of Man"* to refer to himself more than any other title, perhaps because it highlights both his human and divine natures. Here Jesus declares his return as divine King will usher in the fullness of his eternal reign, inaugurated by the final judgment. Jesus had already described himself as the Good Shepherd and shown compassion on those who are like sheep without a shepherd. (See John 10:11 and Matthew 9:36.) Now he compares the final judgment to a shepherd separating his sheep from the goats.

In first-century Palestine, and still today, shepherds typically keep a mixed flock made up of both sheep and goats. During the day the sheep and goats grazed together, but at night they were often kept in different pens. And so, at the end of the day, the shepherd stood at the doorway of the pen and carefully separated the sheep from the goats. Earlier Jesus told two parables describing a mixed nature of the Kingdom which gets sorted out at the end. He said wheat and weeds should grow together and then be separated at the harvest, and clean and unclean fish are caught together in the same net and then sorted out when the fishermen get to the shore. (See Matthew 13:24-30; 47-50.)

Now Jesus explains the criteria by which he will distinguish the sheep from the goats. The sheep cared for Jesus the King by caring for *"the least of these brothers and sisters of mine"* who were hungry, thirsty, lonely, naked, sick, or imprisoned. They are ushered into the eternal Kingdom prepared for them. The goats, on the other hand, did not care for the King by not caring for the least of his brothers and sisters in need. They are cast into eternal punishment while the righteous receive eternal life.

Here Jesus reiterates the inseparable connection he described earlier in the two greatest commandments, loving God and loving our neighbor. (See Matthew 22:36-40) If we love God, we will love his children. It is a mistake to think Jesus is telling us we need to earn our salvation by doing good works for people in need. It is really the opposite. If we know God and love him, we will naturally act in love toward his children, our brothers and sisters.

In another teaching on the final judgment, Jesus said, *"On that day many will say to me, 'Lord, Lord, didn't we prophesy in your name, drive out demons in your name, and do many miracles in your name?' Then I will announce to them, 'I never knew you. Depart from me, you lawbreakers!'"* (Matthew 7:22-23) Good works do not earn God's favor. God's love, forgiveness, and grace are given to us as a free gift. Those who know God by his grace are those who do his will and share in his eternal Kingdom.

Do you know King Jesus? Are you acting in love toward his children? Are you acting as judge toward certain people, or leaving that to the King of kings?

Reflect and Respond
What is Jesus saying to me right now?

What step of faith is Jesus calling me to take today?

Footsteps Every Week: Review

Write a brief summary of what Jesus said to you each day this past week and the step of faith he called you to take:

Monday

Tuesday

Wednesday

Thursday

Friday

Saturday

Footsteps Every Week: Reflect

Big Picture
As you look over what Jesus has said to you this past week, do you see any themes? What is the most important thing you need to remember and believe?

Predictable Pattern
As you look over what Jesus called you to do this past week, is there a new predictable pattern he is inviting you to establish in your life with God and others?

Plant the Word
As you look over the readings from this past week, write out the passage that feels most important for you and memorize it over the next week:

DAY 73

READ AND LISTEN: MATTHEW 26:1-13
Take a minute to listen for what the Spirit is saying in these verses...

COMMENT AND CONSIDER
Jesus concluded his time with the disciples on the Mount of Olives by predicting once more that he was soon going to be crucified. Matthew confirms that prediction by describing the plans which the high priest Caiaphas and certain members of the Jewish council were making to arrest Jesus and have him executed. At that time the office of High Priest was filled by the Roman governor who could appoint or depose at will, which meant that High Priests needed to work closely with the Romans to maintain their position. The average tenure of a High Priest after the time of Jesus was about one and a half years. However, Caiaphas ruled as High Priest for 18 years, which tells you what a savvy politician he was and how closely he aligned himself with Rome.

Against this backdrop Matthew tells us about a banquet held in Jesus' honor in Bethany, where Jesus and the disciples were staying with the extended family of Mary, Martha, and Lazarus. The host of the banquet was a man identified as *"Simon the leper."* This tells us he was probably one of the many "used-to-bes" among Jesus' followers. Some of his disciples *used to be* tax collectors. Some *used to be* prostitutes. Some *used to be* blind or lame. Simon must have *used to be* a leper, because it would be impossible for him to host a banquet if he were still a leper. People with skin diseases had to completely separate themselves from their family and community. No wonder Simon wanted to throw a party to honor the One who healed him and restored him to his family!

John tells us that Lazarus attended this banquet, and that Martha was helping the other women who were serving, but Mary had a different plan. She had a small stone jar of *"very expensive"* perfumed oil, which may have been given to her as part of a dowry. John tells us it was worth nearly a year's wages, roughly the price of a new car today. Mary wanted to honor her Rabbi Jesus with a dramatic act of devotion. (See John 12:1-3)

The men would have gathered in the main room of Simon's house reclining on pillows around a low, three-sided table called a "triclinium," while the women served the meal. Mary slipped in and broke the narrow neck of the alabaster jar containing the perfumed oil and poured it on Jesus' head. In the hot, dry climate of the Middle East, it has always been considered a blessing to wipe soothing oil on your face and hair. It was customary at Jewish banquets for guests to receive a drop of scented oil to rub on their hair. Still today in the Middle East we are often offered a lemon-scented oil to rub on our hands after a meal at a nice restaurant, or even following a dusty bus trip. But Mary went overboard by pouring out this extravagant gift, demonstrating the depth of her love and devotion to Jesus!

It was such a radical act that she was criticized for it, but Jesus defended her, saying this was a prophetic act, pointing to his impending death and burial. And his own prophecy has come true because people all over the world are still talking about what Mary did 2000 years later!

How do you show your devotion to Jesus? Are you extravagant in your expression of love? Are you held back by fear of what others might think or say?

REFLECT AND RESPOND

What is Jesus saying to me right now?

What step of faith is Jesus calling me to take today?

DAY 74

READ AND LISTEN: MATTHEW 26:14-30
Take a minute to listen for what the Spirit is saying in these verses…

COMMENT AND CONSIDER
On the 14th of Nisan in the Jewish calendar, the people of Israel sacrificed lambs at the Temple, and then roasted and served them that night with unleavened bread, bitter herbs, and four cups of wine. This was the annual Passover meal which commemorated the dramatic events by which God saved his people from slavery in Egypt through the blood of the lamb. The host of the meal led his guests through a retelling of the dramatic story of the Exodus as they ate the various parts of the meal and drank from each of the four cups of wine.

Jesus arranged for a secret location to share this final meal with his disciples to ensure he would not be arrested before he could complete his mission. On that Thursday, the Day of Preparation, he sent Peter and John into the walled city with instructions to follow a man carrying a water jar, which was considered women's work. (See Luke 22:7-13.) Once they saw the house where he entered, they were to recite a specific phrase to the owner who would then show them a large upper room where they could prepare for Jesus and the disciples to share this special Passover meal together.

Underneath the traditional location of the Upper Room on the southwest hill in Jerusalem, archaeologists have identified the foundations of a large, first-century Jewish home. There is evidence that, after the Jews were expelled from Jerusalem during the second century and then allowed to return, this house was converted into a public building designed as a place of Jewish-Christian worship, which means this is the first church building ever built for that purpose! In the centuries that followed, larger churches were built on the same site, and today there is an upstairs room built in the 13th century commemorating Jesus' last supper with the disciples.

It was in the upper room of this first-century Jewish home, likely the home of Mary the mother of John Mark, that Jesus gathered that fateful night with his closest disciples. During the meal Jesus predicted one of them would betray him, upsetting the whole group with a heightened sense of foreboding. Then Jesus began to reinterpret the meaning of the Passover meal. They had just eaten the roast lamb which was sacrificed at the Temple when Jesus took a piece of the unleavened bread, prayed the traditional prayer of thanks, and said, *"Take and eat it; this is my body."* Similarly, he picked up the third cup of wine, known as "the cup of salvation," and said, *"Drink from it, all of you. For this is my blood of the covenant, which is poured out for many for the forgiveness of sins."*

It is hard to imagine a more powerful and meaningful picture of what was about to happen. Jesus, the Lamb of God, was about to give up his body and blood as the perfect sacrifice to pay for the sins of the whole world. And now Jesus had given them, and us, a beautiful way to remember and participate in the New Covenant he was about to ratify through his blood shed on the cross. Every time we share this special meal together, we proclaim Jesus' death on the cross for us, and we participate in the powerful forgiveness and oneness that this New Covenant in his blood has made possible, until Jesus returns.

What does it mean to you when you receive Communion? How does sharing in Communion impact your relationship with Jesus and with those in your community?

Reflect and Respond
What is Jesus saying to me right now?

What step of faith is Jesus calling me to take today?

DAY 75

READ AND LISTEN: MATTHEW 26:31-35
Take a minute to listen for what the Spirit is saying in these verses…

COMMENT AND CONSIDER
When Jesus entered Jerusalem, riding over the Mount of Olives on a donkey, he intentionally fulfilled the messianic prophecies, *"On that day his feet will stand on the Mount of Olives,"* and *"Look, your King is coming to you; he is righteous and victorious, humble and riding on a donkey, on a colt, the foal of a donkey."* (Zechariah 14:4; 9:9) As Jesus drew closer to the crucifixion which he repeatedly predicted, I wonder if he also reflected on Zechariah 12:10, *"Then I will pour out a spirit of grace and prayer on the house of David and the residents of Jerusalem, and they will look at me whom they pierced."*

With these prophecies from Zechariah 9-14 fresh in his mind as they walked through the Kidron Valley toward the Garden of Gethsemane, it is no wonder Jesus predicted the disciples' impending desertion by quoting Zechariah 13:7: *"Strike the shepherd, and the sheep will be scattered."* Prophecy is meant to prepare us for what is to come so we can navigate difficult times of testing. Jesus was preparing the disciples to endure the crushing shame of their impending failure. He gave them specific instructions to meet him in Galilee after he rose from the dead, so they could be transformed by encountering him in his resurrected glory and receive the Great Commission.

Jesus was well aware of human frailty, and it was no surprise to him when even his closest friends failed him. In fact, early in his ministry, when he first became popular with the crowds in Jerusalem, John tells us, *"Jesus, however, would not entrust himself to them, since he knew them all and because he did not need anyone to testify about man; for he himself knew what was in man."* (John 2:24-25) Jesus trusted people enough to open himself to them and invite them into close relationship, but he did not put his ultimate trust in them. His trust was ultimately in the Father.

The disciples, however, were woefully unaware of their own frailty. They couldn't imagine deserting their Rabbi in his hour of need. Peter boasted he would be the only one who would be true to his Lord no matter what came. And so, Jesus personalized the prophecy for Peter, predicting he would deny him on three specific occasions that very night. Peter insisted he would rather die than deny Jesus, and all the disciples joined him in overestimating their courage and strength.

As the old saying goes, "the road to hell is paved with good intentions." Jesus comments on his closest disciples' failure in the Garden of Gethsemane by saying, *"the spirit is willing, but the flesh is weak."* (Matthew 26:41) Paul expressed it in his agonized words to the Romans, *"For I do not do the good that I want to do, but I practice the evil that I do not want to do."* (Romans 7:19) It is not enough that we want to do the right thing; we also need the power to act on our intent, particularly when to do so will cost us in some way.

The only way we will overcome the shame of our failure and follow the risen Jesus is to die with him on the cross and rise with him in new life. This is Paul's testimony: *"I have been crucified with Christ, and I no longer live, but Christ lives in me."* (Galatians 2:20) Are you aware of your own frailty? Are you learning to die to yourself and walk in the power of the risen Jesus?

REFLECT AND RESPOND

What is Jesus saying to me right now?

What step of faith is Jesus calling me to take today?

DAY 76

READ AND LISTEN: MATTHEW 26:36-46
Take a minute to listen for what the Spirit is saying in these verses…

COMMENT AND CONSIDER
During this final Passover week in Jerusalem, Jesus and his disciples stayed with Mary, Martha, and Lazarus in Bethany on the other side of the Mount of Olives. Each morning they walked 1.75 miles over the Mount of Olives, down into the Kidron Valley, and up to the Temple Mount. Sometimes, perhaps when it was too late to go all the way back to Bethany, they stayed on the Mount of Olives. That Passover was one of those late nights, so Jesus and the disciples went to a place called Gethsemane at the base of the Mount of Olives to spend the night.

Gethsemane means "place of olive pressing," because it was an olive orchard with installations for the production of olive oil. When you visit Gethsemane today, you find a small grove of ancient olive trees tended by Franciscan monks, some of which are over a thousand years old! They don't date back to Jesus' time as some claim, because Josephus records that the Romans cut down every tree on the Mount of Olives when they besieged Jerusalem in AD 70, but they are the oldest in the world. Next to this ancient grove is a cave which has been converted into a chapel. Archaeologists have discovered there the remains of a first-century olive press which may have been the very place Jesus and the disciples stayed when they slept on the Mount of Olives.

This is where Jesus settled his disciples for the night, took three of his closest disciples for support, went a stone's throw away among the olive trees, and began to pour out his heart to the Father. It is important to note that, even though Jesus had already predicted the impending desertion of all his disciples and Peter's triple denial, he still asked his closest friends to come with him and pray. If Jesus knew he needed the support of his imperfect friends to face the challenge ahead, how much more do we need each other!

Jesus' prayer is a model for us to imitate. In his full humanity, Jesus desperately wanted to avoid the terrible suffering that lay ahead. He did not hide this human desire or put on a religious façade like the hypocrites he so recently criticized. Instead, he was brutally honest with his heavenly Father, begging him three times to *"let this cup pass from me."* But he concluded each prayer with a declaration of absolute surrender, *"Yet not as I will, but as you will."*

We should remember that at any point Jesus could have simply slipped over the ridge of the Mount of Olives and disappeared into the night. He spent 40 days in the desert wilderness just to the east and could easily have found a cave in Wadi Qelt where no one would ever find him. And yet Jesus overcame this temptation to escape his fate and succumb to his own desires. When he rose from his third prayer, Jesus was filled with angelic strength (see Luke 22:43) and the authority of someone who knows who he is and is completely surrendered to the will of his Father. From this point all the way to the cross, Jesus never wavered in his conviction and determination to fulfill his mission.

What do you do when you are tempted to give up on God's will? Who do you ask for support when faced with overwhelming obstacles? How do you pray when you desperately want to avoid what God seems to be calling you to do? Jesus shows us the way.

Reflect and Respond
What is Jesus saying to me right now?

What step of faith is Jesus calling me to take today?

DAY 77

READ AND LISTEN: MATTHEW 26:47-56
Take a minute to listen for what the Spirit is saying in these verses…

COMMENT AND CONSIDER
Although the Romans ruled Jerusalem with a garrison of soldiers in the Antonia Fortress, they allowed the Jewish religious leaders to keep a security detachment of their own to enforce rulings of the Sanhedrin. They also allowed a force of Levitical Police to protect the holy precincts of the Temple. However, these Jewish security forces were not allowed to wield swords, but instead used clubs to enforce their will. The Roman Governor also assigned a contingent of Roman soldiers to the religious leaders, upon whom they could call when more force was needed.

When Judas arrived at Gethsemane that night, a *"large mob with swords and clubs was with him from the chief priests and elders of the people."* That means Caiaphas and his allies had dispatched, not only their own security forces, but also some of the Roman soldiers assigned to them by Pontius Pilate. Earlier in the week Judas had made the fateful decision to sell out his Rabbi for thirty silver coins. While they were still in the upper room, he left the meal to inform the authorities of Jesus' whereabouts. Most likely Judas first brought the soldiers to that house on the southwest hill of Jerusalem and then, realizing Jesus had already departed, he took them to their usual spot on the Mount of Olives.

Judas Iscariot was one of Jesus' twelve full-time disciples. The descriptor "Iscariot" indicates he came from the Jewish town of Kerioth in southern Judea. Jesus had entrusted the finances of their ministry to him, which means Judas was one of his most trusted disciples. (See John 12:6.) It was customary for Jewish men in the first century to exchange a kiss on the cheek as a warm greeting between friends. It is a bitter irony that Judas chose this sign to identify Jesus to the soldiers. Even in the face of this terrible betrayal, which came as no surprise to him, Jesus still called Judas *"friend."*

By contrast, when he saw what was happening, Peter drew one of the two swords they kept to protect themselves on the road from bandits. He took a swing at Malchus, one of Caiaphas' slaves, and narrowly missed his head, slicing off his ear. Matthew doesn't mention that Jesus healed the man's ear, but he does record Jesus' rebuke of Peter. Jesus knew he was going to be arrested and executed, and he went to great lengths to make sure it didn't happen before he could complete the teaching and training the Father had called him to do. But now he knew the time had finally come.

Jesus willingly submitted to his fate when he could have resisted arrest. In fact, he told them there were twelve legions of angel warriors at his disposal, which means Jesus could have called 72,000 heavenly soldiers to protect him. It is like that time the Aramean armies had surrounded the Prophet Elisha in Dothan, but he was not afraid because he could see the army was surrounded by fiery chariots of angelic warriors ready to fight for him. (See 2 Kings 6:8-23.)

Jesus taught his followers that, when they were conscripted to carry a Roman soldier's gear the required one mile, to offer a second mile as well. He taught them, when someone punched them in the face, to offer the other cheek rather than punch back. Now he walked the talk by willingly submitting himself to unjust arrest and punishment.

To what injustice is God calling you to submit without fighting back? How can you take up your cross and follow Jesus today?

Reflect and Respond

What is Jesus saying to me right now?

What step of faith is Jesus calling me to take today?

DAY 78

READ AND LISTEN: MATTHEW 26:57-68
Take a minute to listen for what God is saying in these verses…

COMMENT AND CONSIDER
The Sanhedrin was the Jewish religious council of Jerusalem comprised of 70 members drawn from the powerful priestly families of Jerusalem (*"the chief priests"*), the wealthy aristocratic families of Jerusalem (*"the elders"*), and the trained experts in the Law (*"the scribes"*), plus the High Priest who presided. The chief priests were primarily aligned with the party of the Sadducees, and the scribes included elite members of the Pharisees. The Romans put them in charge of the religious and civic matters of the Jewish community. They normally met in the Chamber of Hewn Stone, a hall built into the inner courts on the Temple Mount.

The night Jesus was arrested, the soldiers took him to the house of the High Priest Caiaphas where a select group of the Sanhedrin had gathered for the express purpose of condemning Jesus to death. The exact location of this house is not clear, although it was somewhere on the southwest hill where archaeologists have identified many wealthy priestly homes. The traditional location with the most credibility is located on the site of an unfinished Armenian Orthodox church just outside the present-day Zion Gate in the southern wall of Jerusalem, but it has not yet been excavated to verify this claim.

The illegitimacy of this trial is made clear by the fact that they were not meeting in their official court, that the trial was held in the middle of the night, and that the Sanhedrin actively solicited false testimony. Even so, they had trouble getting just two of these false witnesses to agree. Finally, two managed to agree on the lie that Jesus had threatened the destruction of the Temple. In fact, Jesus had accurately predicted its coming destruction by the Romans. (See Matthew 24:2.) When the High Priest demanded a response, Jesus refused to defend himself.

Finally, the High Priest asked Jesus directly if he was the Messiah. Jesus replied, *"You have said it."* Then he went on to apply to himself two messianic passages which he had been debating with them in the Temple courts: the description of the heavenly Son of Man (see Daniel 7:13–14) and the reference to the divine figure who sits at the right hand of God (see Psalm 110:1–2). His claim of divinity was crystal clear. Jesus was telling the council that the next time he saw them, he would be returning as the divine King to fully establish his reign on earth.

The High Priest tore his robes, the traditional sign of grief or condemnation, and cried out, *"He has blasphemed!"* Blasphemy was speaking against the sacred name of God, which included a false claim of divinity. The penalty under Jewish Law was death. (See Leviticus 24:16.) However, the Sanhedrin did not have the power to execute criminals, and a Jewish charge of blasphemy did not warrant the death penalty in a Roman court, so the High Priest had to convince Pilate to condemn Jesus on some other basis.

The contrast of Jesus' innocence with the corrupt manipulation of these religious leaders is impossible to miss. Although they tried to condemn Jesus, they really indicted themselves. What are you willing to do to get what you want? How do you respond when others threaten your security and power? Who have you falsely condemned to feel more secure?

Reflect and Respond
What is Jesus saying to me right now?

What step of faith is Jesus calling me to take today?

Footsteps Every Week: Review

Write a brief summary of what Jesus said to you each day this past week and the step of faith he called you to take:

Monday

Tuesday

Wednesday

Thursday

Friday

Saturday

Footsteps Every Week: Reflect

Big Picture
As you look over what Jesus has said to you this past week, do you see any themes? What is the most important thing you need to remember and believe?

Predictable Pattern
As you look over what Jesus called you to do this past week, is there a new predictable pattern he is inviting you to establish in your life with God and others?

Plant the Word
As you look over the readings from this past week, write out the passage that feels most important for you and memorize it over the next week:

DAY 79

READ AND LISTEN: MATTHEW 26:69-75

Take a minute to listen for what the Spirit is saying in these verses…

COMMENT AND CONSIDER

Although all the disciples abandoned Jesus after his arrest and fled, two regrouped to follow Jesus and the soldiers back to the house of the High Priest Caiaphas. Matthew tells us one of them was Peter, and John tells us he was the other. John says he had a connection to Caiaphas' household that allowed him to gain access, so both ended up inside the courtyard of the very house where the religious leaders were putting Jesus on trial. (See John 18:15-16.) We have to give these guys credit for some serious bravery!

The traditional location for Caiaphas' house has not been excavated, but a large palatial mansion has been excavated in the same neighborhood. It covers about 6500 square feet with multiple levels, making it the largest and most luxurious private home from first-century Jerusalem discovered to date. It has two beautifully constructed ritual baths which, along with the furnishings and decorations, identify it as the home of a wealthy priestly family. Furthermore, it has a large central courtyard and a spacious upper room looking down into the courtyard, which fits the description of Jesus' trial. If this was not the house of Caiaphas, his would have been very like it.

As Peter entered the courtyard of this fancy house, the doorkeeper identified Peter as a follower of Jesus, but Peter immediately denied it. While Jesus was on trial in the large upper room, Peter was below in the central courtyard, warming himself around a charcoal fire with some of the slaves and staff members. In the glow of the fire, another woman pointed him out as a disciple of Jesus, but Peter swore and said, *"I don't know the man!"*

Finally, some others identified Peter's Galilean accent as a dead giveaway for someone who was with the Prophet from Galilee, but Peter vehemently denied it, cursing and making oaths. Just then he heard the rooster announcing the coming break of dawn, and like a knife piercing his soul he remembered the prophecy Jesus had spoken over him, *"Before the rooster crows, you will deny me three times."* Peter broke down under the weight of his failure and shame and left the house of Caiaphas weeping bitterly.

All of us can identify with Peter. We want to stand with Jesus. We plan to represent him well. But when the moment comes and we feel the possibility of rejection, our courage often falters. It is so easy to hide our faith. It is so hard to speak up when the opportunity to talk about Jesus arises. A profound spiritual battle is at work within us, as our flesh desperately resists being identified with Jesus. The enemy of our soul exploits this weakness and does everything he can to keep us quiet about our faith.

The good news is Jesus understands. In fact, he knows we will fail, and his grace is sufficient for us. The risen Jesus found Peter in his failure and shame and reinstated him as the leader of the disciples. Peter preached the first sermon on the day of Pentecost and went on to become a powerful, Spirit-filled apostle who brought the Good News of the Kingdom to the ends of the earth. Jesus loves to use frail vessels like us to convey his extraordinary treasure.

How have you failed to represent Jesus to others? What have you learned from that? How will you allow the Spirit to build in you the same courage and boldness Peter learned to exercise?

Reflect and Respond

What is Jesus saying to me right now?

What step of faith is Jesus calling me to take today?

DAY 80

READ AND LISTEN: MATTHEW 27:1-10
Take a minute to listen for what the Spirit is saying in these verses…

COMMENT AND CONSIDER
Matthew tells us Judas approached the Chief Priests, offering to betray Jesus to them for a price. They weighed out thirty silver coins, and he accepted. (See Matthew 26:14-16.) This is the exact phrase Zechariah used in his prophecy depicting the wages of a shepherd leading his flock to slaughter: *"So they weighed my wages, thirty pieces of silver. 'Throw it to the potter,' the Lord said to me—this magnificent price I was valued by them. So I took the thirty pieces of silver and threw it into the house of the Lord, to the potter."* (Zechariah 11:12-13) Here we have yet another prophecy from Zechariah 11-14 pointing to the tumultuous events of these final days of Jesus' life on earth!

It is confusing that Matthew attributes this prophecy to Jeremiah, when no such passage is found in that biblical book. This may be based on the way the Hebrew Scriptures were organized in antiquity, in which the scroll of the Prophets began with Jeremiah, so the entire scroll could be referenced by the name of the first prophet, Jeremiah. In any case, Matthew shows us how this prophecy was fulfilled in surprising detail: the amount the religious leaders paid Judas for his betrayal, the fact that Judas led Jesus to the slaughter, how Judas then tried to give the money back to the priests in the Temple, and that ultimately the money paid for a potter's field.

As we noted earlier, Jesus trusted Judas enough to turn over the financial management of the disciples to him. He gave him a seat of honor at the last Passover supper and included him in the meal they shared together, although he knew Judas was going to betray him. Even in the moment of his betrayal, Jesus called Judas *"friend."* Why would Judas want to betray Jesus? On the surface it seems he was greedy for silver. Yet once the deed was done, Judas was so remorseful he returned the money and committed suicide.

Some have wondered if Judas was disillusioned because Jesus didn't fulfill the expectation of a military Messiah who would overthrow the Romans and establish an independent Jewish state. It was becoming clear Jesus was doing the opposite; he intentionally confronted the temporal powers and willingly submitted himself to death at their hands. Perhaps Judas tried to force Jesus' hand by putting him in a position where he would have to use his supernatural power to save his own life. Perhaps Judas counted on Jesus calling upon those twelve legions of angels to overthrow the Romans.

Whatever Judas' motives, all these events certainly had a dark spiritual side to them. The devil was at work through sinful people and corrupt systems, seeking to destroy the Light of the World before he could accomplish his mission to save the world by inaugurating God's Kingdom of love and grace. Luke and John tell us Satan entered Judas and used him as the instrument of Jesus' death. (See Luke 22:3 and John 13:27.) Little did the devil know that this death would be the very means of Jesus' victory!

It is significant that Judas is never recorded calling Jesus "Lord," but only "Rabbi." Perhaps this is the problem. If we only see Jesus as our Teacher, it is easy to try and use Jesus for our own ends. But if we truly submit to him as our Lord and King, then we have to let go of our agenda and trust that his way is always the best. Are you using Jesus or submitting to him?

Reflect and Respond
What is Jesus saying to me right now?

What step of faith is Jesus calling me to take today?

DAY 81

READ AND LISTEN: MATTHEW 27:11-31
Take a minute to listen for what the Spirit is saying in these verses…

COMMENT AND CONSIDER
Pontius Pilate was appointed Governor of Judea by Emperor Tiberius at the recommendation of Lucius Aelius Sejanus in AD 26. Since a Roman governor's primary job was to keep the peace so goods and taxes kept flowing back to Rome, Pilate avoided any action likely to provoke a reaction from the people, especially when the crowds gathered in Jerusalem for festivals. In AD 31 Pilate's patron Sejanus fell under suspicion of treason, so Emperor Tiberius had Sejanus executed. This put Pilate in a precarious political position, making him even more susceptible to political pressure from the Jewish religious leaders at the time of Jesus.

Pilate's headquarters were in the impressive city of Caesarea on the coast, but for the festival of Passover he moved into the huge palace Herod built on the western hill of Jerusalem. The religious leaders brought Jesus here to convince Pilate to condemn Jesus to death. Archaeologists have excavated the remains of Herod's Palace and discovered it was comprised of three strong defensive towers built into the western wall of the city and two large buildings with a huge plaza in between. This plaza was known as the *"gabbatha,"* which is Aramaic for "pavement." (See John 19:13.) At either end of the plaza stood a raised platform called the *"bema"* where Pilate stood before the crowd with Jesus. It was on the *gabbatha* before this *bema* that the religious leaders gathered a crowd of people they had coached to call for Jesus' crucifixion.

Although the Sanhedrin had condemned Jesus for blasphemy, they knew this was of no concern to the Romans, so they brought a charge tailored to evoke the death penalty. By accusing Jesus of claiming to be a king, they framed him as a revolutionary seeking to overthrow Roman rule, a clear capital offense in the eyes of Rome. When Pilate asked Jesus directly, *Are you the king of the Jews?"* Jesus responded obliquely, *"You say so."* As the religious leaders poured out their accusations against Jesus, he did not respond.

Throughout his trials Jesus refused to defend himself against false accusations, knowing it would be pointless. But when he was asked directly about his identity, Jesus affirmed he is the divine Son of God who has come to take the throne of David and establish God's eternal Kingdom of justice and peace. Years later Paul quoted an early Christian saying in a letter to his young disciple Timothy, *"For if we died with him, we will also live with him; if we endure, we will also reign with him; if we deny him, he will also deny us; if we are faithless, he remains faithful, for he cannot deny himself."* (2 Timothy 2:11-13)

As Pilate examined Jesus, he became increasingly convinced of his innocence. His wife had a prophetic dream affirming Jesus' righteousness. Pilate recognized the religious leaders were trying to manipulate him into eliminating their rival. He tried to pass the buck to Herod Antipas, ruler of Jesus' home region Galilee, but that didn't work. He offered to release Jesus as a Passover amnesty, but the crowd called for the release of the notorious terrorist Barabbas instead. Finally, he caved to the political pressure and, in order to preserve his own position and power, condemned an innocent man to death, ordering him to be scourged and crucified.

How are you being pressured to compromise what you know is true, so you don't rock the boat? Have you slipped into the trap of affirming a lie to preserve your position and power? How can you avoid making Pilate's mistake?

Reflect and Respond
What is Jesus saying to me right now?

What step of faith is Jesus calling me to take today?

DAY 82

READ AND LISTEN: MATTHEW 27:32-44
Take a minute to listen for what the Spirit is saying in these verses…

COMMENT AND CONSIDER

When Pilate condemned Jesus to death by crucifixion, the soldiers took Jesus into a different part of Herod's Palace, stripped and tied him to a post, and began lashing his bare back with a scourge. This whip made of strips of leather imbedded with metal and bone tore flesh from the victim's back, exposing ribs and even organs. After the soldiers mocked his "royal attire," they laid a heavy cross beam across his torn shoulders and began to lead a grisly procession through the streets of Jerusalem heading for Golgotha. They processed north from the Palace of Herod to the Gennath Gate (Aramaic for "garden"), where they exited through the western city wall.

After the Jews returned from exile in Babylon under the Edict of Cyrus in the sixth century BC, they cut large limestone blocks from the hill on the west side of Jerusalem to rebuild the Temple. Eventually this rock quarry fell into disuse, was overgrown, and in the first century BC it was converted into a beautiful garden cemetery, with tombs cut into its rock walls. When the sixth-century BC builders cut stone from the quarry, they came to a section of limestone that was fissured and unstable, not suitable for building. So, they simply quarried around that section, leaving a 20-foot-high rocky outcropping which the Romans later adopted as their place of execution.

This rock was just outside the city wall and close to the main road leading to the coast, so it provided the visibility the Romans wanted to terrify the population with their torturous executions. Because of the bone-colored rock and its terrible function, this rocky outcropping came to be known as *"Place of the Skull,"* or *"Golgotha"* in Aramaic. Archaeologists have confirmed that the ancient Church of the Holy Sepulcher is built over the site of this ancient rock quarry. When you go to the church today, you can visit the Chapel of Golgotha and actually touch this grisly rock with your own hands.

Archaeological discoveries have illuminated the Roman method of crucifixion. The victim's arms were tied or nailed through the wrists to the cross beam, which was hung on the vertical post, to which their feet were then nailed through the heel bones. As the victim hung on the cross, the weight of their body pulled down on their arms, constricting the muscles around the lungs, which slowly began to fill with fluid. As their breaths became shorter and shorter, the victim had to pull himself up to breathe, pulling against the wounds in their wrists and heels while scraping their bloody back up and down against the rough wood of the post. The cross was essentially a self-torturing device on which its victims slowly suffocated to death.

As Jesus hung on the cross enduring this torture, the sign nailed above his head read, *"This Is Jesus, the King of the Jews."* Those who passed by challenged him to prove this was true by coming down from the cross. All three groups of the religious leaders who had orchestrated his execution joined in the mockery, ridiculing his claim to be the messianic Son of God and pledging to believe in him if he could only exercise supernatural power to save himself as he saved so many others. Even the criminals who were being executed with him joined in the derision, perhaps as a diversion from their own torment.

How does Jesus' suffering on the cross illuminate the kind of King he is? What does it mean for you to follow him by taking up your cross?

Reflect and Respond

What is Jesus saying to me right now?

What step of faith is Jesus calling me to take today?

DAY 83

READ AND LISTEN: MATTHEW 27:45-56

Take a minute to listen for what the Spirit is saying in these verses…

COMMENT AND CONSIDER

As Jesus hung on the cross, his breaths got shorter, and it was harder for him to push up and get more air into his lungs. As his life began to slip away, the whole creation seemed to groan with him in agony. Darkness covered the land in an ominous sign that the Light of the World was about to be extinguished. Mark tells us Jesus was crucified about 9:00 AM (*"the third hour"*) and now, six hours later, Jesus was near the end. (See Mark 15:25, 33.) In a reminder of his full humanity, Jesus cried out to the Father in his native language, *"My God, my God, why have you abandoned me?"* This was surely an expression of the depth of his suffering, but it was not a cry of hopelessness or defeat.

To biblically literate Jews, it was obvious Jesus was quoting the first line of Psalm 22 in which David described suffering in strikingly parallel terms to what Jesus endured, including details such as his hands and feet being pierced, the soldiers casting lots for Jesus' clothes, and being surrounded by those who mocked and derided him. Although the first half of Psalm 22 describes agonizing suffering such as this, the second half of the Psalm is filled with praise to God for his faithfulness and prophetic declarations such as the final line, *"They will come and declare his righteousness; to a people yet to be born they will declare what he has done."* (Psalm 22:31)

It is true Jesus experienced all the emotions that come with profound human suffering, but he also proclaimed his trust in the Father and hope in God's power to redeem all of humanity through his death on the cross. When Jesus breathed his final breath, that redemptive power was dramatically unleashed. The huge 30-foot-tall curtain in the Temple that separated the Holy of Holies from the Sanctuary was suddenly torn from top to bottom. Jesus' death is the perfect sacrifice which rendered the sacrificial system of the Temple unnecessary and makes it possible for us to *"approach the throne of grace with boldness"* because we have been forgiven and made right with God. (See Hebrews 4:14-16.) Jesus foretold this moment when he designated the cup of salvation at the last supper as *"my blood of the covenant, which is poured out for many for the forgiveness of sins."* (Matthew 26:28)

When Jesus died the earth shook, and tombs around Jerusalem were opened. When Jesus rose from the dead three days later, the power of his indestructible life brought back some of those who had died, just as he was able to raise Talitha and Lazarus during his ministry. These events were so dramatic and the witness of Jesus on the cross so profound that it broke through the cynical hearts of the last people we would have expected: the battle-hardened centurion and the soldiers responsible for Jesus' execution. Whether they understood all the theological implications or not, their testimony rightly identified this crucified teacher, healer, and prophet as *"the Son of God!"*

For over 2000 years the cross has been the enduring symbol of faith in Jesus. What does Jesus' death on the cross mean to you? Can you comprehend a love so great that God would set aside his infinite power and majesty to be humiliated, tortured, and executed on a cross to save you for himself? Are you ready to let God take away your sin, shame, and fear so you can learn to live the life you are meant to live?

REFLECT AND RESPOND

What is Jesus saying to me right now?

What step of faith is Jesus calling me to take today?

DAY 84

READ AND LISTEN: MATTHEW 27:57-66
Take a minute to listen for what the Spirit is saying in these verses…

COMMENT AND CONSIDER
Joseph was a wealthy member of the Sanhedrin who came from a city in Judea called Arimathea. According to John, he was friends with another wealthy member of the Sanhedrin, a Pharisee named Nicodemus. They both had come to believe in Jesus but kept their faith hidden for political expediency. (See John 19:38-42.) Now Joseph stepped out of the shadows and courageously identified himself with Jesus, even though Jesus was now branded an executed criminal and enemy of Rome. Joseph had recently commissioned a new family tomb be dug into one of the walls in the same ancient rock quarry where Jesus was executed. He went to Pilate, asking for Jesus' body, offering to use his new tomb for the burial.

In the first century, Jews who could afford it built rock-cut tombs for their extended families. Typically, these tombs had a low entrance that could be sealed with a stone and that gave access to a burial chamber with either shelves or slots cut into the walls where bodies could be laid. When someone died, their body was washed, anointed with oil and spices, and wrapped from head to toe with linen cloths. The body would be laid on one of the shelves or slid into one of the slots, and then the tomb was sealed with a stone plug. In the case of a more expensive tomb, the door was sealed by a rolling stone shaped like a disk and fit into a slot that allowed the stone to cover the doorway.

One year later after the flesh had decayed, the family returned to remember their loved one. The tomb was opened, and the bones were gathered and placed in a small stone bone box called an ossuary, which would be stored in the tomb. Over the years generations of family members' remains accumulated in their family tomb. The Gospels are clear that Joseph's tomb was new, and no bodies had ever been buried in it before. And so, Joseph and

Nicodemus prepared Jesus' body, laid it on the burial shelf, and rolled a large stone in place to seal the tomb.

The next day, although it was a Sabbath, the religious leaders were so worried their troubles with Jesus were not over that they came to Pilate and asked that the tomb be sealed and guarded so no one could falsely claim Jesus had risen as he foretold. Eager to put this whole situation behind him, Pilate agreed and ordered a detachment of soldiers to place an official seal over the rolling stone to secure the tomb. This seal was comprised of a cord attached at each end to the rolling stone and the outer wall of the tomb by wax imprints to make certain the stone was not tampered with. This, along with the armed guard, would ensure no one could steal Jesus' body and claim he had risen from the dead.

Joseph was convinced Jesus was a rabbi worth following, but not enough to risk his position and reputation. He was still hedging his bets. When Jesus died on the cross, something changed in Joseph that made him willing to risk everything in order to be faithful to his Lord and King Jesus.

What kind of a disciple are you? Do you believe in Jesus, but not enough to risk your comfortable lifestyle or the approval of others? What would it take for you to identify yourself with Jesus as your King? Maybe you need to stand at the foot of the cross and consider what it means to be a true follower of Jesus.

REFLECT AND RESPOND
What is Jesus saying to me right now?

What step of faith is Jesus calling me to take today?

Footsteps Every Week: Review

Write a brief summary of what Jesus said to you each day this past week and the step of faith he called you to take:

Monday

Tuesday

Wednesday

Thursday

Friday

Saturday

Footsteps Every Week: Reflect

Big Picture

As you look over what Jesus has said to you this past week, do you see any themes? What is the most important thing you need to remember and believe?

Predictable Pattern

As you look over what Jesus called you to do this past week, is there a new predictable pattern he is inviting you to establish in your life with God and others?

Plant the Word

As you look over the readings from this past week, write out the passage that feels most important for you and memorize it over the next week:

DAY 85

READ AND LISTEN: MATTHEW 28:1-15

Take a minute to listen for what the Spirit is saying in these verses...

COMMENT AND CONSIDER

Ancient Judaism had no such thing as women disciples. Only boys were educated in the synagogue school system, and only men were accepted as apprentices to rabbis. And yet Jesus consistently affirmed the equal value and dignity of women. Even more radical was Jesus' recognition of women as his disciples, whether it was Mary of Bethany taking the posture of a disciple, or the women who were included in the family of disciples. (See Luke 10:38-42 and Matthew 12:48-50.) Of all the women who followed Jesus in Galilee, Mary Magdalene was clearly the leader. Having been powerfully delivered by Jesus from seven demons, she was listed with the wealthy aristocratic women who followed Jesus and helped fund the mission. (See Luke 8:1-3.)

Mary Magdalene is consistently named first when the Gospel writers list Jesus' female disciples by name, and she stood with Jesus' mother at the foot of the cross when Jesus died. Matthew tells us that *"many women"* along with Mary Magdalene witnessed Jesus' death and watched as Joseph and Nicodemus sealed Jesus' body in the tomb. All four Gospels name Mary Magdalene first when they tell of the women's determination to venture out before dawn on that Sunday morning to return to the tomb and anoint Jesus' body.

Although Matthew only mentions two, five named women went to the tomb early that morning: Mary Magdalene, Mary the mother of James the younger and Joses, Salome the mother of James and John the sons of Zebedee, Joanna the wife of Chuza, and Susanna, plus several other unnamed women. (See Mark 16:1; Luke 24:10.) When they arrived at the tomb, the stone had been rolled away, and guards were nowhere to be found. After first assuming Jesus' body had been stolen, they then encountered an angel who announced Jesus' resurrection. But it was when they met the risen

Jesus face to face that everything changed! The same Jesus they had seen nailed to a cross, hung up to die, and sealed in a tomb was now gloriously transformed and fully alive, never to die again! It was not a vision, it was not over-active imagination, it was not a carefully concocted conspiracy. They saw him, they talked to him, they touched him, and they worshiped him.

All doubt was gone, and it was crystal clear Jesus really is who he claimed to be—the incarnate Son of God, the divine Son of Man, the Messiah King who has come to set his people free and establish an eternal Kingdom of love, joy, and peace! The resurrection of Jesus changed everything. Now they knew everything Jesus ever said was true. Now they knew Jesus had the power to fulfill every promise he ever made. His death on the cross paid the price for their sin, and his resurrection from the dead broke the power of death, hell, and the devil. Although the religious leaders bribed the guards to spread the rumor that Jesus' body was stolen, from this point on the disciples who encountered the risen Jesus knew the truth. Jesus was really alive!

The fact that women were credited as the first witnesses of the resurrection while the men reportedly hid in fear tells us this was not a story someone made up. The fact that so many who saw Jesus alive again were tortured and killed for that testimony tells us their testimony is true. Who would die for something they knew was a lie? What does it mean for you that Jesus really did rise from the dead? How can your testimony impact others?

REFLECT AND RESPOND

What is Jesus saying to me right now?

What step of faith is Jesus calling me to take today?

DAY 86

READ AND LISTEN: MATTHEW 28:16-20

Take a minute to listen for what the Spirit is saying in these verses...

COMMENT AND CONSIDER

Although the female disciples were the first to encounter the risen Jesus, later that evening the male disciples also met him in the upper room on the southwest hill of Jerusalem. Others met him on their way to Emmaus and came back to Jerusalem that night to confirm this news with the rest of Jesus' followers. The following Sunday Jesus appeared to the disciples again in the upper room, and this time Thomas was there to share the experience.

Amidst all this excitement, they did not forget that Jesus instructed them to return to Galilee where he would meet them. And so they did return, and Jesus facilitated another miraculous catch of fish before cooking them breakfast on the beach. We don't know all the other times Jesus met with the disciples, but we know on one occasion over 500 people were present at the same time to see Jesus alive! (See 1 Corinthians 15:6.) We know he met with his brother James. Over a period of forty days, Jesus spent time with the disciples, they worshiped him, and he opened their minds to the Scriptures.

Despite these incredible experiences, Matthew tells us some still doubted. This is a reminder that no matter how many incredible things we might witness, we all have to come to Jesus on the basis of faith. It is always a question of whether we are willing to trust him enough to put our lives in his hands.

Then Jesus gave the disciples his final commissioning before ascending back to his eternal position as a member of the Trinity at the right hand of the Father. This Great Commission begins with the transfer of authority. Although Jesus gave his disciples authority to heal and cast out demons earlier in his ministry, now Jesus had risen from the dead to conquer sin, hell, death, and the devil! It was the triumphant Jesus who transferred to his followers *"All authority… in heaven and on earth."* This is the basis of the Great Commission, that we have been authorized to represent Jesus by acting and speaking on his behalf.

The specific commissioning Jesus gave was for them to continue doing what they learned as they followed him in Galilee. *"Make disciples of all nations."* Making disciples means inviting people into our lives and calling them to follow the Jesus-shaped example they see in us. Baptism in the name of the Trinity is the entry point to this new way of life and this new family of God. But the process of discipleship is ongoing training to live a life that looks like Jesus and produces the same kind of fruit he produced.

Jesus concluded the commission with the promise that, by the indwelling presence of the Holy Spirit, he will be with us no matter where we go, giving us the power to do God's will on earth as it is in heaven! When the day of Pentecost came shortly after Jesus made this promise, the Holy Spirit was poured out on the disciples, and they became powerful apostles sent out to bring the Good News of the Kingdom to all the nations of the world. They built Jesus-shaped spiritual families on mission, which came to be called "churches." They reached the lost and made disciples by inviting people into their spiritual families and investing in their lives just as Jesus had done for them.

Have you received the commissioning Jesus gave to his disciples? Are you willing to give your life for this great calling as they did?

Reflect and Respond

What is Jesus saying to me right now?

What step of faith is Jesus calling me to take today?

Footsteps Every Week: Review

Write a brief summary of what Jesus said to you each day this past week and the step of faith he called you to take:

Monday

Tuesday

Wednesday

Thursday

Friday

Saturday

Footsteps Every Week: Reflect

Big Picture

As you look over what Jesus has said to you this past week, do you see any themes? What is the most important thing you need to remember and believe?

Predictable Pattern

As you look over what Jesus called you to do this past week, is there a new predictable pattern he is inviting you to establish in your life with God and others?

Plant the Word

As you look over the readings from this past week, write out the passage that feels most important for you and memorize it over the next week:

MORE RESOURCES BY BOB ROGNLIEN TO HELP YOU FOLLOW JESUS

Find them all at www.bobrognlien.com

- **Books** | Footsteps Every Day: Mark, Luke, John
  - Continue the journey you have begun with daily Gospel readings and reflections on the Way of Jesus, illuminated by insights from history, archaeology, and culture. These three books of daily devotions together with the current volume can take you through all four Gospels in one year.

- **Book** | Recovering the Way: How Ancient Discoveries Help Us Follow the Footsteps of Jesus
  - An in-depth treatment of Jesus' life illuminated by the history of his time, the cultural background of his world, and archaeological discoveries from our time. Includes over 100 photos, reconstruction drawings, and maps. Excellent for serious students and teachers who want to go deeper.

- **Book** | The Most Extraordinary Life: Discovering the Real Jesus
  - A shorter telling of the true story of Jesus from his baptism to his resurrection, informed by history, archaeology, and culture. Each chapter begins with an expanded account of an event from Jesus' life which reads like a historical novel. Written for everyday people who know Jesus and those who want to get to know him for the first time.

- **Video** | Recovering the Way: The Video Series
  - An in-depth video teaching series that illuminates the life of Jesus with thousands of full color photos, reconstruction drawings, and animated maps. The twelve 45-minute episodes

correspond to the twelve chapters in the book, *Recovering the Way* (see above) and will bring the Way of Jesus to life for you.

- **Trip | The Footsteps of Jesus Experience**
  - A 14-day journey through Israel and Palestine, following the life of Jesus from birth to resurrection. We keep the group relatively small, stay in unique Christian guesthouses, drive ourselves in vans, do lots of walking off the beaten path, focus on the historically verifiable sites, and keep an intentionally spiritual focus. It is not a tour, but an intensive pilgrimage.

- **Podcast | The Footsteps Podcast with Bob Rognlien and Matt Switzer**
  - In each episode Footsteps Experience leaders Bob and Matt take you on a journey to a significant site in the Holy Land and show how the discoveries there bring a specific biblical passage to life with new insights and applications.

- **Trip | The Footsteps of Paul Experience**
  - A 15-day journey from Antioch to Corinth through Turkey and Greece, following the missional journeys of the Apostle Paul and his disciples. We keep the group relatively small, stay in boutique hotels with historical and cultural charm, drive ourselves in vans, go off the beaten path, focus on the historically verifiable sites, and keep an intentionally spiritual focus. It is not a tour, but an intensive pilgrimage.

- **Book | A Jesus-Shaped Life: Discipleship and Mission for Everyday People**
  - A practical guide to putting the Way of Jesus into practice in your everyday life with the people who are closest to you. It tells the story of how Bob and Pam learned to pattern their lives and their family more intentionally after Jesus. It

also offers practical tools, vehicles, and strategies to make discipleship and mission a part of your daily life.

- **Book | Empowering Missional Disciples**
  - A resource for leaders who want to help those they lead to live a life that looks more like Jesus and produces more of the fruit he produced. Includes lots of field-tested tools and vehicles for multiplying missional disciples.

www.ingramcontent.com/pod-product-compliance
Lightning Source LLC
Chambersburg PA
CBHW051943290426
44110CB00015B/2094